Parenting Teenagers

Parenting Teenagers

Bob Myers

Jessica Kingsley Publishers
London

Line drawings by Julie Smith
Cover illustration by Julie Smith
Edited by Bronwyn Collie
Designed by John van Loon

First published in 1992 in Australia by
The Australian Council for Educational Research Ltd,
Radford House, Frederick Street,
Hawthorn, Victoria 3122, Australia

First published in the United Kingdom in 1996 by
Jessica Kingsley Publishers Ltd
116 Pentonville Road
London N1 9JB, England

British Library Cataloguing in Publication Data
A CIP catalogue record for this book is available
from the British Library

ISBN 1-85302-366-3

Printed and Bound in Great Britain by
Biddles Ltd, Guildford and King's Lynn

CONTENTS

With special thanks to Jean and Ron Quick.

CHAPTER 1

AN OVERVIEW OF ADOLESCENCE

Introduction

*P*arenting Teenagers in the 1990s was written in response to the need for a simply-worded guide for parents who are experiencing difficulty in their relationship with their adolescent children, or who want to improve that relationship. In saying 'their' adolescent children I do not mean that the ideas, methods and examples presented here can only be used by the old, traditional two-parent family. In fact, so many teenagers now live in single-parent families or in families where there is one step-parent, or de facto parent, that the traditional family is becoming something of a rarity. The term 'parent' is used throughout this book as a matter of convenience but should be taken to include any of the persons mentioned above; the information presented here can be used by any person who is fulfilling, or trying to fulfil, the role of a parent. Indeed, by altering the wording only slightly the same ideas can be used by residential youth workers and social workers.

While we are on the subject of convenient terms, I have used many of the terms people commonly use when they talk about their offspring, such as kids, children, young people, young adults, teenagers and adolescents, partly because this *is* how people talk and partly because some of the topics and methods apply to *all* people, not just teenagers, and the wording at times will reflect this.

Parents who are finding it difficult to cope with the behaviour of a child seem to need two things, and to need those two things quickly:

1   They need to understand why the child is behaving in such a way;
2   They need to feel confident in their way of handling the situation.

Parents sometimes think they will go crazy trying to work out a child's behaviour, what they can do to control the situation, and how they can correct the behaviour. Sometimes parents come to believe that their child needs psychiatric help because they find it so hard to make sense of the behaviour. It often does not help much to ask the child to explain the behaviour because most children, especially adolescents, seem to limit their answers to all such questions to either, 'Dunno', or, 'It was something to do, I was bored'. Many people come to doubt their worth as parents at this stage of their parenting, and wonder what has gone wrong. 'Where did I go wrong?' and 'I know I'm not perfect but I didn't think I was that bad either' are two expressions of bewilderment commonly heard from parents having problems with their teenage children.

For some parents the difficulties experienced in the parent–child relationship go way back to the early years and become worse at adolescence. If this is how it has been for you, you may need to seek professional help. This doesn't necessarily mean psychological or psychiatric help; it may be as simple as a talk with your doctor about the child's general health, or about his diet. Many children act up badly after eating certain

foods, especially those which contain artificial additives. Perhaps you could take note of any change in behaviour which occurs after eating or drinking junk foods, for instance, which usually do contain artificial additives. There are books available which list food additives and their effects, and which tell you how to recognise the additives in a product by the numbers on the label. This subject will not be mentioned again but it is well worth keeping in mind.

In the next chapter I will attempt to provide some understanding of why kids misbehave. Some quite simple suggestions will be put forward there and in later chapters, which you may wish to try in your own way in order to gain confidence in your handling of adolescent behaviour. For now though, I just want to set the scene, to talk in general terms about being a parent of adolescent children.

A stage of turmoil and change

The adolescent stage of parenting takes many parents by surprise, and leaves them wondering what on earth is going on. It is a stage that requires you to change your parenting methods to match the changes your children are going through. It requires using your old parenting skills in new ways and realising that you already have the skills to cope, that you just need to become more aware of them. I hope to help you realise that you are the expert on your family's problems and that in the end you know more about how to deal with them than any outside 'expert'.

So this book is about helping you to cope with this special stage of parenting, by making practical suggestions about all kinds of situations. You will become aware of parenting skills you didn't know you had and remember many from earlier years that you will again find useful. After all, you by now *do* have many years experience in parenting and of course you once went through adolescence yourself.

Parents, then, are the experts on their families. No-one can ever know the problems of a family like its members and each member has the capability of working towards solving problems which arise. All that parents need are the tools to help themselves and other family members find the solutions. In this book I will discuss some ways of dealing with problems and how to put these into action.

Adolescence is somewhat different to all other stages of parenting. Nevertheless, there are similarities between the adolescent stage and earlier stages, in particular the 2-year-old stage, so much so that some parents find it useful to think of adolescents as two year olds with muscles. Thinking back to how they coped with the defiance and independence of that stage, they simply adapt their methods to suit the defiance and independence of the adolescent. Take care in using this method, however, because it usually doesn't work if your way of dealing with the two year old was to give her a hefty smack — the two year old with muscles may just thump you back.

One of the most striking similarities between an adolescent and a two year old is the way an adolescent will push the rules to see how far they will bend, to see just how much he can get away with. Remember how the two year old used to watch you and give you a cheeky grin as she held a finger just off the thing she was told not to touch? The adolescent is doing the same, that is, testing the limits so he gets to know what behaviours people will accept before blowing their stack. This can be extremely annoying for parents, but the child really does need to find out what the sensible limits are now that she is changing into a young adult. The child is also moving into a different social scene and needs to find out what behaviours will be tolerated outside the home. To do this she may test the limits to see if they really are the limits or if people will accept a little more.

Limits and how to set them will be discussed more fully later. For now it is enough to say that limits that are either too strict or too loose will result in big trouble. Fortunately, there are some simple guidelines that will help you set workable limits. Again, these will be discussed in later chapters.

Two year olds and adolescents both experience major changes in their lives, which they must learn to cope with. For example, two year olds can now walk, and so they have to learn where they are allowed to walk and where it is not permitted, where it is safe to walk and where it is dangerous. They are also beginning to talk, and will have to learn what are acceptable and what are unacceptable words. While they have to be taught to say 'please' and 'thank you', it seems they need no prompting to pick up 'bad' words. Children this age are also discovering how to get their own way, by tantrums or by sweetness, and if they are to use these new skills wisely, they must be aware of the consequences of what they do, that is, they must learn which behaviours pay off and which ones do not. And change is what adolescence is all about, on the physical, emotional, and psychological levels.

Parents expect their adolescent children to change physically, and generally this does not cause too much hassle. It is suffice to say that boys and girls learn to adapt to these changes, but need your guidance. Changes in attitude, however, may come as a surprise to you, and may even directly oppose what you yourself believe. In more extreme cases parents may think they have 'failed' to bring up their children 'properly'. It may be hard to pinpoint when or why changes in thinking came about because, unlike physical changes, changes in thinking are 'invisible'. However, at adolescence, changes in thinking are just as great as bodily changes and, like the latter, guidance is needed, though it may not always be welcomed.

The very young child sees his parents as knowing

everything and being capable of doing anything. His parents are always right and always know how to go about things. To the young child there is only one right way to do things, and that is the way his parents do them. The child learns to do as his parents do. But then the unthinkable happens. The kid who always listened and always did as she was told turns into an adolescent who thinks her parents know nothing. What has happened is that the thinking powers of the child have changed, she is now capable of seeing that her parents' way of doing things is only one way, that there are other ways and some of these may be better than what her parents do. The child can even think up new ways of her own, and these may be better than her parents' ways as far as she is concerned. This new monster seems to throw all her parents' values out the window when it suits her, but is capable of supporting them brilliantly when arguing against someone, if that suits her. An adolescent's new found skills in logical thinking are matched only by her ability to abandon logic when she is in danger of losing an argument, and this naturally leaves her parents feeling somewhat bewildered.

The adolescent needs to test out his new thinking skills and learn how to control them. He will make mistakes and learn from them, just as he has learnt to use and control other skills in the past. And, when he won't listen to your words of caution, maybe you will just have to let him find out the hard way, just as you did when he was a two year old, even when you knew it may hurt him a little.

Knowing how and when to let go

The adolescent will desperately need her new thinking powers because she is moving into a world of drugs, sex, conflict, job search, unemployment, love, in short pressures and uncertainties of all kinds, and is trying to establish her independence at a time when she needs a huge amount of guidance to cope with all these things successfully. She is equipped with the ideas and values that you have passed on, but now needs to find out what her own ideas and values are. Most adolescents do this through intense involvement with their peer group, so they can assess the values and ways of living they are used to against others' values and lifestyles. The conflict between needing support and needing independence is partly why adolescents are so unpredictable, why they may alternate so rapidly between mature behaviour and absolute childishness. Indeed, it is quite common for parents to talk about their adolescent children as 'being like two different people'.

If you can put together your years of parenting skills with an understanding of the behaviour and misbehaviour of your teenage children, you will experience more of the enjoyment that can go hand in hand with the anguish of being a parent to adolescents. Even the most painful part of adolescence, the fact that your child is breaking away from you, can become an enjoyable event and form the basis for the next stage of parenting. This time of 'letting go' is rather confusing for both the parents and the young person, and there is next to no information on how to cope with it. You can read advice that tells you that you must let go of the kids, but how do you do this successfully? How much do you let go and at what rate? The final chapter in this book will look at how this 'letting go' can be done at a rate you will feel comfortable with.

So while the adolescent wants more freedom, his parents are probably applying the brakes. While the adolescent is pushing to become an independent person, 'trying out his wings', his parents wish to slow the process through fear that he will rush headlong in and come to some harm. The adolescent, however, may well think the brakes are there simply to stop him from having fun. It is as though kids will always want more freedom than they can handle, and their parents will always try to keep them below what they can handle. The struggle to break free, then, is a natural process which is hard for both parents and children. Parents find it difficult to judge how much to let the brakes out, and no matter what they decide it is never enough for the child. The child finds it difficult because she cannot ask her parents for advice, because they are the ones she is trying to convince she can look after herself. Teenage kids don't want to be seen anywhere near their parents, let alone admit that they are dependent on them. Parents often misunderstand this attitude, believing they have a poor relationship with their children, when this may not be the case at all.

Adolescence is a passing stage in the job of being a parent. For most parents and adolescents the turmoil and problems of this time will fade fairly quickly, although there are always some relationships which will take a severe battering. Parents who take the trouble to read books like this and genuinely seek solutions still suffer a little, but they have a lot going for them, not so much from what they read, but because they care enough to seek out knowledge. Adolescents need that caring even though their desire for independence may prevent them from showing it, and may even make it difficult at times for parents to show their love.

Children now know their rights

As if all the above wasn't enough, there is the fact that kids now tend to be well aware of their rights. Many parents become worried and confused when they hear some of the interpretations about the rights of children, especially those around such things as the United Nations Convention on the Rights of the Child. Many people interpret the Convention as removing the right of parents to pass on values and beliefs to their children; it seems that it becomes the right of the government to decide what will or will not be taught to children, and that parents must just tow the line. Schools are teaching children their rights and children are coming home to tell their parents how they can and cannot treat them.

Many parents are disturbed by these things and may feel that they are losing control. It might seem to them that they can no longer discipline their children, that their children are allowed to do as they like, have whatever friends they wish, see whatever movies or read whatever books they want, have complete freedom to come and go as they please, and not be punished for anything. Of course these sorts of interpretations are rubbish and can only cause unnecessary problems. Children's rights become something to fear, something to be hidden from the child.

Schools *are* teaching kids their rights, and so they should. Kids are entitled to know their rights and have them respected. However, many kids, its seems, are prone to believe some of the 'rubbish' about their rights and will deliberately twist the truth to take advantage of their parents' fears in order to gain that bit more freedom. This is only natural, any kid worth his salt will be trying to gain extra freedom, and having a Bill of Rights for kids is heaven sent, especially when his parents haven't got a clue about it.

Australia's laws are more in line with the Convention than those of the countries that originally prompted it. Australia has comprehensive and meaningful laws to protect children's rights and in general has got rid of legislation that in the past meant that abused children were treated like criminals. One effect of this has been the removal of the legislation that quite a lot of parents used as a threat to get their kids to behave. Threats of being made a ward of the State, for example, of being put in a 'home' to learn some discipline or taken to court for being 'in moral danger' are fast losing their effect.

Added to all this, however, is what seems like a contradiction because while the laws are reflecting the trend towards the rights of children, they are also reflecting the trend towards the parents being made more responsible for the control of their children. Parents are expected to have greater influence over the behaviour of their offspring, yet they can no longer rely on the law for their authority. Parents may well feel that they are on their own in trying to influence their children, and that they are not well protected from people who try to undermine that influence. We will return to this apparent contradiction in the final chapter to see how it can be resolved.

Coping with the rights of the child

In days gone by parents believed that they had God-given authority over their children, which meant that they expected their offspring to obey the rules they set down. Imagine how frustrated these parents would become now if they asked their daughter to do something and were told to 'shove it'. Where would they go from there? Probably pick up a big stick and give her a lesson in the art of gentle persuasion. We will deal with this again in chapter 8 but for now the good news for parents is that they *do* have God-given influence over their children, an influence that is quite easy to identify but takes a great deal of practice to exert effectively. In other words, it is easier to say than to do.

A good relationship with their children is all parents need to resolve the issues surrounding such things as the Convention of Rights and changing legislation. If a good relationship exists between parents and their kids no outside laws matter. In a good relationship the people involved know and respect each other's rights. Rights only become an issue when an individual believes his rights are being ignored, and there is likely to be big trouble in the relationship if he believes his rights are being constantly ignored. As parents you should not worry about the United Nations Convention or about legislation on child protection. You should simply concentrate on improving your relationship with your children, and arguments about rights will never arise.

But before I go on I want to make it clear what I mean by 'relationship'. The subject of human relationships is far too complex to go into very deeply here, so I will narrow things down a bit by considering only a few points about relationships. First of all I am going to set aside all blood relationships because they remain the same regardless of their quality. A father–son relationship remains a father–son relationship even when they are beating each other to death; an uncle you have never met remains your uncle and it is impossible to change that relationship.

NO FAMILY IS THE SAME

Nowadays, as noted earlier, there is a growing number of families in which the members are not all blood-related. The background of some families includes marriage, divorce, remarriage and so on, often with children being produced from each union. Or it could be marriage, divorce, de facto, separation and so on, but the results are the same. It means there are many people who are trying to parent children to whom they are not blood-related, and that there are also many children who may be having trouble coping with this situation.

The parent of the child or the parent to the child?

These special parents generally experience extra problems because they are not the 'real' mother or the 'real' father. But, as noted earlier, when I talk about parent–child relationships I include these parents as well, the ones that are trying to fulfil the parent role under what can be very trying conditions.

Parents of adopted children may also have added difficulties. All adolescents experience turmoil and uncertainty as they try to figure out who they are and how they fit into the world. The adopted child must also deal with these issues, but they tend to be aggravated if she does not know her real ancestry. Many adopted children feel they do not 'fit in' because of this. The anxiety caused by not wanting to hurt her adoptive parents, plus the guilt about her urge to find her real parents, doesn't help much either. Children can act out badly from this type of pressure.

The adopted child can be used as a good example of what I mean when I talk about a relationship. The real mother–child relationship is impossible to change even though the real mother may have given the child up for adoption at birth, and someone else has been mother to that child ever since. The natural mother is the mother *of* the child but the adoptive mother is the mother *to* the child. The natural mother has the distinction of being part of an everlasting mother–child biological relationship that the adoptive mother can never have with the child, but the adoptive mother can have a good mother–child parenting relationship that the natural mother is unlikely ever to have.

So while it is easy enough to be the mother or father *of* a child, it is quite a different matter to be a mother or father *to* a child. The latter implies a relationship which can be good or bad depending on how much work goes into it. So whenever I refer to a relationship I mean one that is obtained through effort, the 'mother to' kind of relationship.

The above comments can refer to any relationship. For instance, while it is easy enough to claim to be a friend *of* someone, every now and then you may be called on to be a friend *to* that person. The same comments also apply to that minefield called the husband–wife relationship.

We tend to judge a relationship on how 'at ease' and free of tension we feel in the company of another. The tensions present between a parent and an adolescent, however, can be part of a healthy readjustment in the relationship, and do not necessarily mean that the child is less in need of his parents' approval. Indeed, at the adolescent stage, it is extremely important to have that approval, although the child may make it difficult to find much to approve of at times.

The teenager's need for approval

One of the major driving forces of adolescence is the search for belonging. Belonging and, therefore, approval are partly satisfied by the acceptance of the peer group, and will probably be more fully satisfied in intimate relationships later on. The adolescent finds herself in the midst of the move away from home, the search for a life partner and new family to belong to for the rest of her life, but this does not lessen the need for approval from her own parents.

Children of all ages want the approval of their parents and this is so strong that it even applies to most of those who have been abused, those who have the most reason to not want anything to do with their parents. Children must be protected from real neglect and/or abuse, and sometimes this means they have to be removed from their parents' home altogether. However, it would still be unwise to assume that the child's attachment to, and need for his parents, is any weaker because of this.

Many, many children who have been taken from the family home because they are the victims of constant abuse continue to desire a normal relationship with their parents, and show obvious delight when the parents show any kindness towards them, or even briefly contact them. This applies to abused adolescent children just as much as to smaller children. The adolescent may refer to her mother as 'the old hag', but then write very moving poems about the unreturned love she feels for her. Likewise, young people who have been abused by their father usually still want healthy contact with him.

Summary

Parenting at the adolescent stage requires a change in the methods used by parents but the skills gained at earlier stages can be adapted to the new situation. There are many similarities between the adolescent stage and the 2-year-old stage because of the changes which take place, especially when it comes to testing out rules and showing independence. Patience is needed as values are tested in the peer group and both parents and teenagers will undergo the pain that the natural process of breaking away brings.

Parents must cope with behaviour which results from all manner of causes, from diet to changing legislation, and the sometimes mischievous interpretations of the rights of children. The main thing parents need to worry about is their relationship with their daughters and sons; if this is strong, problems can be worked through. Conflicts may make it difficult for parents to see and respond to adolescents' need for attention and approval but this need is also the parents' God-given helper.

CHAPTER 2

THE PURPOSES BEHIND MISBEHAVIOUR

Children learn how to control their parents

In chapter 1 I mentioned that there are two things that parents need, and need quickly, when they are having problems with a child's behaviour: they need to understand the reasons behind the behaviour, and they need to feel confident in their way of handling the situation. I also commented on how useless it usually is to ask kids to explain their behaviour because they just say 'Dunno'. Another problem with asking for explanations is that the child then has an opportunity to think up an excuse that appears to justify the behaviour. If a child gets the idea that his parents accept this, the same reason may be used over and over again, whenever he gets caught: 'But last time you said . . .'. This can become a real problem because children are generally fairly quick to quote the last time a particular excuse was accepted and claim that, because it was accepted once, it must always be accepted.

If this happens to you, you can challenge your child by saying something like, 'Just because I once made the mistake of accepting that excuse doesn't mean that I have to make the same mistake again'. Or, 'Yes, I did accept that excuse last time but I am not bound to accept it twice'. Or, 'I don't have to accept the same excuse twice, just as you could have chosen not to do that twice'.

The relationship between reason, cause and purpose

To avoid misunderstandings it is important that certain key words I use here be understood in the way I mean them. Every now and then I will stop to explain exactly what I mean by certain words and their relationship to each other. Three words that need some explanation at this stage are: 'reason', 'cause' and 'purpose'.

A *reason* can be thought of as the 'why', whatever it was that motivated the behaviour. The reason is either *from a cause* or *for a purpose*. For the reason to be 'from' a cause means that the cause is something in the past that led to the behaviour occurring. The cause may only be a few seconds into the past but it is still in the past. To say that a reason is 'for' a purpose then, means that the purpose is an aim for the future, even if it is only a few seconds into the future. The purpose is something that is to be gained from the behaviour, something which may or may not happen.

The most likely reason a child uses a particular behaviour to achieve a particular purpose is because that behaviour has achieved that purpose in the past. This means that there is usually a mixture of both a cause and a purpose in the behaviour:

Example one: If a child wants a drink and has found in the past that a tantrum will draw the parents' attention to that fact, the child is very likely to throw a tantrum.

Example two: If a child wants to draw parental attention away from something, the child may attract attention to herself by throwing a tantrum.

In the first example the purpose is to get a drink, and the cause of the behaviour is that the behaviour has worked previously when the child has wanted a drink. This is probably the very first thing most children learn about the art of controlling their parents.

In the second example, the reason for throwing the tantrum is probably still due to the past success of throwing tantrums, but the purpose is not what it appears to be. The child's purpose is not attention-getting for herself but rather to distract her parents from noticing something else, probably the evidence of another bit of misbehaviour.

Shortly we will look at a fairly easy method of working out why a child is misbehaving and how you should respond to it. For that method to work, however, you must first accept that all human behaviour has a purpose, even when this may not be clear or the person may not be conscious of his intentions. The purpose of all behaviour is to satisfy some need or want; this applies to all people, not just to children. When I scratch my nose it is because I need to get rid of an itch; my comfort has been disturbed by the itch, so I scratch to restore my comfort. Admittedly, I might scratch out of habit, in which case I do not need an itch to scratch. Even so, the act of scratching was originally motivated by an itch. 'Not so', you say, 'perhaps it was copied from someone'. True, but this is still not contrary to the idea that actions are motivated by needs, because the very act of copying is usually motivated by the need to be like someone else.

Even when we do something for someone else, we do it to satisfy some need of our own. This may appear to deny the existence of love, and to say that we are simply selfish in all our actions, but this is certainly not what I mean. Mother Theresa of Calcutta is selfless in her service to others, yet it can still be said that she acts to satisfy a deep need of her own, her deep need to serve God. This example should be kept in mind when I say that all behaviour is ultimately to satisfy our own needs.

We gain pleasure from helping others, or giving to others, and when we do things for our loved ones the pleasure we get from our actions can be very great indeed. We may also experience the pain of rejection, yet we may still act to satisfy our need to meet our responsibilities. And children are the same, they act to satisfy some need or want and use whatever methods have worked in the past to gain that satisfaction. If a tantrum works more effectively than being nice, then a tantrum it is.

THE REASONS ARE DEEP IN THE PAST...

Just as I have asked you to accept that all human behaviour has a purpose, I also ask you to accept that people will use old and proven ways of achieving that purpose. Therefore, as I said, the cause of their behaviour is in the past and usually deep in the past. If we accept that there is a cause for all behaviour, can we go back and do anything about it? The answer is no.

Child psychologists will tell you that a child may start off using what she has been told is a 'nice' way of getting what she wants, only to resort to a good old tantrum when nice methods fail; way back at babyhood she learnt that having a tantrum is the best way to get results. This is fine, but there is no way that knowing this is going to make it any easier to deal with a tantrum here and now.

In the next chapter I will talk more about how the past affects the present and the future, although you don't have to dig too deeply to find the clues that tell you why a child is misbehaving in the way that he is. Indeed, one only needs to look at the immediate purpose behind particular misbehaviour, and give some thought to whether this is often the purpose of a child's misbehaviour. If the purpose of a child's misbehaviour is generally the same, then this provides the clue to what is going wrong with the parent–child relationship.

The examples given in the last few pages encompass the first things all children learn about the art of controlling their parents. Over the years a child learns how her parents will respond to all sorts of behaviour, and learns how certain behaviour can be used to control her parents. A 15-year old child has 15 years experience at controlling his parents, and 15 years experience at anything is a lot of experience. A person who has 15 years experience at a job is due for long-service leave and is by then generally considered to be pretty good at the job. When the kids reach 15 it is the parents who are looking for long-service leave. The child's control of her parents may continue until the parents realise just what is happening and decide to regain control of the situation by changing their usual way of reacting to some behaviour.

The first step in breaking the child's control is for the parents to recognise the reasons for the behaviour. As we go into later chapters you will see that the other thing you must become aware of is how you usually react to certain behaviour.

The four purposes of misbehaviour

In this section I have adopted the method of recognising the purposes behind misbehaviour from the American program, Systematic Training For Effective Parenting of Teens (STEP), to suit our situation. It is important to keep in mind, how-ever, that this is only one way of trying to understand children's misbehaviour. I use it because it is fairly simple, and because most people can relate to it. Under this method misbehaviour is seen as belonging to one or more of the following four categories:

1   Power
2   Attention
3   Revenge
4   Inadequacy

It is considered that the main purpose of a child's mis-behaviour is to stir up a particular feeling in his parents and he is generally successful in this. He has studied his parents for some time now and is accurate in assessing their response and effective in achieving his purpose. However, his accu-racy and effectiveness can be used by his parents to decide which of the four headings his behaviour comes under. Parents can get to know the purpose behind certain behav-iour by taking note of what feelings have been stirred up, and by being aware of the child's continued attempts to stir up those feelings again.

Power, attention, revenge, inadequacy

Power

If the feeling the behaviour stirs up in you is anger, it is quite likely that a power struggle between you and your child is taking place. The exchange between you may follow a pattern something like the following: The child does some-thing that you get angry about, you angrily respond to the behaviour, and this prompts another action from the child that ensures your anger will continue. The child's action is a form of defiance and a challenge to you to do something about it. Your response is your attempt to do something about the child's defiance, but the child simply defies your effort.

In this process, the purpose of the misbehaviour is to get you angry and the probable cause is that the child is angry about some restriction she sees as unfair or unnecessary. She wants to do whatever it is but can't get permission from you. So she must either miss out or defy you, back down or damage the relationship. This is a real bind for both of you because you are in the same situation, the child has made sure of that by doing something she knows will get you angry.

Example one: Your child argued long and loud to be allowed to stay out until 1.30 a.m. but you eventually laid down the law and said that 10.30 p.m. is the limit. The kid arrives home well after the time you told him to be in, so you angrily tell him that he is grounded for a week. He leaves you seething by promptly turning around and going out again, just to show you that you can't stop him.

Example two: A daughter thinks her mother has no right to say who she can and cannot have as friends. She knows that her mother will get upset if she talks about wanting to see a particular boy, so she talks about the boy until her mother finally explodes and forbids her ever to see him again. The daughter then declares, 'I will pick my own friends and you can't stop me', and storms out of the house.

The power struggle isn't always rowdy, though, because it is quite possible for a kid to defy his parents very quietly. He may, for example, simply not do what his parents want. No fuss, no drama, no nothing. The quiet type of defiance can be just as maddening as the rowdy type. The child may do what you want while you are watching but as soon as your back is turned he stops.

Attention

If the feeling that the child stirs up in you is annoyance and your response only incites further annoying behaviour, the purpose of the child's behaviour is to get your attention. The latest term for this type of behaviour is 'acting out', but I still think 'attention-seeking' is more appropriate.

For example, your daughter keeps interrupting you when you are talking to someone and so you become annoyed.

You tell her to go away and stop bothering you. She then either continues to annoy you in the same way, or starts some other annoying behaviour. Or you may be reading a book and your son keeps asking questions until you get annoyed and close the door on him. He might then turn his music up very loud, start to sing loudly or perhaps just keep knocking on the door and saying silly things. Whatever he does, his actions are meant to keep you aware that he is still around. It doesn't really matter what the behaviour is, you will simply find that a great deal of your time is spent attending to it. The feeling of annoyance may develop into anger and, usually, the annoying behaviour will stop when anger is shown. There may then be a short period of peace before some other annoying behaviour starts.

Revenge

You can assume that revenge is the purpose of a child's behaviour if his actions make you want to hurt him in some way. Your response to the urge to hurt him brings on more misbehaviour so that you feel you want to get even, again by hurting him in some way.

For example, your child deliberately breaks your favourite cup. Your feelings are a mix of hurt and resentment so you get even by calling her 'clumsy' or 'stupid'. The child reacts to this by scratching a photo of you with a nail. You punish the child for this but later find that your car keys have vanished. This time you decide that the punishment has to be a real beauty, so you tell her she has just missed out on her holiday in Fiji. That night your car vanishes. There is one other thing that you can safely assume, that the child also feels a mix of hurt and resentment.

Inadequacy

If you feel inadequate, helpless or powerless in the face of your child's behaviour, and whatever you do about it just brings on more behaviour of a similar kind, then it is most likely that the child also feels helpless and inadequate.

This is probably the most difficult of the four purposes to understand and accept. It can also be very difficult to detect, even though it is very common among all age groups. It is also a very difficult one to explain because there are so many variations and the signs of it may be very subtle. In some way, however, the child will not accept responsibility for his behaviour and will pass the blame on to anyone or anything other than himself. The blame may be passed on to you, for example, and in such a way that you actually feel you are to blame. Hence your feelings of inadequacy, or helplessness, because it seems you are unable to do anything about the problem.

For example, a child may appear to have a dejected and helpless acceptance of a situation that she feels she has no control over. This may be shown as boredom and the responsibility for the boredom may be put on to you, and you feel helpless to do anything about it.

On the other hand, the denial of blame can result in very defensive behaviour, even to the point of aggressiveness. A child may simply be passing blame on to another person or thing or he may be desperately avoiding taking responsibility for his behaviour.

Regardless of what form it takes, the purpose behind the behaviour is to stir up feelings of inadequacy or helplessness in you and is the result of the child believing that she is at the mercy of life, that she has no control over what happens to her. The child will try to get his parents to accept responsibility for whatever happens to him, for knowing where his favourite shoes were left, for his best jeans not being dry in time for the disco, for cleaning up his bedroom, indeed, for anything that suits him. Children have really studied their parents for this one, and tend to be very successful in getting them to accept responsibility for a great deal of their misbehaviour.

One of the reasons we find it so difficult to see the purpose behind this behaviour is that we all tend to make excuses for or deny responsibility for our behaviour. We therefore tend to accept excuses from others in the hope that they will accept excuses from us; it is a convenient 'trade-off'.

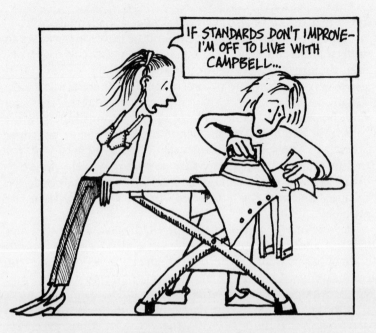

How you can react to misbehaviour

There is one all-important point to keep in mind when attempting to cope with misbehaviour: the only thing you have any real control over in any situation is yourself, and it is through control of your own actions that you will gain control over the general situation. Just as you cannot control the behaviour of others, they cannot control your behaviour. Your daughter cannot *make* you do anything, even though she may have learnt in the past that you will always respond to particular behaviour in a certain way. So she does such-and-such and, predictably, you react in the usual way. You allowed her to control you by doing exactly what she expected.

So the secret in how to handle a difficult situation is to recognise what the other person expects you to do and to then do something different, if you want to. You already know different ways of handling situations and, if you think about it, you can decide to respond in an unexpected way.

Most people, for instance, would undoubtedly use a different method of handling being stirred up by a 10-foot-tall Hell's Angel than they would use if a two year old was the one causing the trouble.

Everyone seems to know a few different ways of handling awkward situations but few seem to realise that these different ways can become *deliberate actions*, rather than mere reactions. In other words, you can regain control of a situation by choosing your reaction. When you are deciding how to handle a situation, I strongly suggest you resist the temptation to say what you think is the purpose behind the behaviour. To say something like, 'You are just doing that for attention' is very likely to cause more trouble than you've already got. Following are a few suggestions that may help just for now.

How to react to a power struggle

In a power struggle between a parent and a child, one appears to win and the other appears to lose. But really both lose because the relationship is damaged. A power struggle is like a war in that one side or the other wins, but both sides suffer. And the one that loses may choose bigger weapons in the next fight or become more determined to tough it out.

The only way to successfully handle a power struggle is to take charge of the situation by backing off. I do *not* mean backing down and giving in. I *do* mean taking control by removing yourself from the conflict and leaving the child with no-one to compete with. You must then do only those things that you have full control over. You should not attempt to have the last word because you are withdrawing from the contest. Three options available to you are:

1 You can state your opinion and state what you intend to do about the situation (make sure it is something you are willing to do and fully able to follow through with) and then refuse to argue about it.

2 You can state your opinion, state that you are willing to talk about it when the child is willing to listen to your side, and then withdraw from the conflict.

3 You can state that you are willing to agree to disagree.

Regardless of what you decide to do, it is important to withdraw from a power contest with a child, because you cannot win it. Even if you appear to win by getting the child to give in, the relationship will be damaged and the child may be pushed towards choosing different weapons to help him win the next battle.

How to react to attention-getting

The best way of dealing with attention-getting behaviour is to ignore it. This can be extremely difficult because this sort of behaviour can be very unnerving, and the very act of ignoring it may cause the child to act even worse. This is because attention-seekers cannot stand being ignored and will sometimes go to extreme lengths to regain attention.

I found one girl who constantly sought my attention particularly annoying one day. She had been unsuccessfully trying to command my attention in several ways and then decided to empty an ashtray into the water I was washing dishes in. I simply emptied the sink and refilled it with fresh water and detergent. She again emptied an ashtray into the water. I again refilled the sink. The next lot of water had a packet of breakfast cereal tipped into it. I refilled the sink. Through all of this she was calling me names and making insulting remarks as she flitted in and out of the kitchen. I had not spoken one word all the while. When the breakfast cereal didn't work, the girl burst into tears, ran into her room and went to bed. When she emerged from the room after a good sleep, I made a point of talking at length with her, but the above incident was not mentioned.

Ignoring attention-getting behaviour can be very difficult but it is still the most effective way to gain control of the situation. At the same time, however, you must keep in mind that the child who is trying to gain attention is very likely to be in need of attention. So it should be given, but at a time when you think it is more fitting, and not when the attention is actively sought. Attention on demand, whether in response to positive or negative behaviour, is best avoided.

The ways a child will seek attention are endless and can range from constant little arguments to downright dangerous behaviour. It can be anything at all that will hold your

attention on the child, and this may be so called good behaviour or so called bad behaviour. For instance, a child may be doing all sorts of good things and running to show them to you, or wanting you to look at what she has done. Good behaviour as attention-seeking can be just as irritating as bad behaviour.

If it looks as though a child is likely to come to some harm in trying to get attention when being ignored, it may be wise to start giving extra attention at times when he is not demanding it. Of course you should attend to dangerous behaviour, but only enough to prevent or treat the damage. This may mean doing whatever is necessary while remaining completely silent.

The important point then, is that children do need a lot of attention and should get it when they are acting in an ordinary, acceptable manner and not when they are seeking it. This will let them know that they do not have to be extra good or extra bad to be noticed and to belong.

How to react to revenge

Revenge runs in cycles and there are three important things to keep in mind about these cycles:

1   Someone has to do the first hurtful thing;
2   The second person has to know what will hurt back;
3   The original hurter has to hurt again.

The cycle is generally set in motion when a parent unintentionally hurts a child. As a result the child is hurt, or resentful, or a mixture of the two. Perhaps the child is hurt because you did not go to a school function, or you may have embarrassed her in front of her friends. Perhaps it was because you divorced her father.

In the second part of the cycle the child wants to hurt the parent back and, from years of studying the parent, he knows exactly how to do it. Now, if his mother continues to get upset, as she has in the past when a particular subject is raised or word used, the child can control how his mother feels. A child doesn't have to hit you to hurt you, all he has to do is hint about smoking dope or leaving school. It might be name-calling, like calling you a slut, that gets you going. Whatever it is, you can be sure that your reaction in the past has told him it is a sure way of getting at you if he wants to. The point is that the child needs to know what will hurt you and if his behaviour is not succeeding in hurting you, he will have to change tactics.

This brings us to the third part of the cycle, with you feeling a natural urge to hurt the child back in some way. This urge must be resisted at all costs; you must stop yourself from doing what you first feel like doing. I put it like that because the revenge cycle has to be broken by someone or it will get steadily worse and cause grave damage to the relationship. You can take control of the situation by not reacting in the way the child expects, thereby preventing the cycle from growing stronger.

Once you have stopped the natural urge to hurt back, think about why the child is trying to hurt you. If your natural reaction is to get your own back on her for something, isn't it likely that she is also trying to get you back for something? If the child is trying to hurt you, you can be sure of one thing, that she feels hurt herself. Maybe this is not justified, but that doesn't really help. Perhaps you are totally unaware that you have hurt the child, and would never deliberately do so anyway. Maybe the child is hurt because you haven't noticed his name in the paper for best and fairest at footy. Or maybe he wants to get back at you for not being his real father.

One very common reason for a child seeking revenge against a parent derives from a feeling of resentment about the unevenness of the power in the relationship. She may not be able to do anything to gain more equal power but she sure can try to get even by hurting, or damaging, or abusing, or by insults. Giving a child more say in making decisions about things that affect him may help to even up the power problem. However, to do this effectively you *must* be willing to allow his opinion to carry weight in decision-making.

Sometimes it is fairly difficult to decide whether you are dealing with a power struggle or revenge because the two are quite similar. It may be helpful to keep in mind that revenge is more the result of losing face by backing down in a power struggle.

How to react to inadequacy

The way feelings of inadequacy are most often invoked is by blaming some behaviour on other people or things in order to avoid the consequences of one's actions. So, the way to handle the situation is to make sure that the child accepts responsibility for his actions by taking the consequences of them. This is how we all learn that what we do controls what happens in the future. No excuses or apologies should be accepted; accepting an apology is the same as accepting an excuse, and sets the stage for repeated misbehaviour and repeated apologies. What should follow any misbehaviour is the consequence of that misbehaviour, a consequence that cannot be avoided by apologising. Anyway, most apologies are just a quick, 'Sorry about that, didn't mean it'. This of course means absolutely nothing, especially when it is used often. A genuine apology, however, is a different thing altogether and can be accepted, even if it doesn't contain a promise not to misbehave again. A genuine apology is given by a person who realises that her behaviour has caused some problem and she expresses regret that the problem was caused. A genuine apology goes something like: 'I believe that your feelings were hurt by my actions and I regret that. I don't regret doing what I did but I am sorry that you are hurt'. It may also be: 'I regret that my actions hurt you. I can't promise that I'll never do that again, but I will never deliberately hurt you'.

A particularly annoying thing about quick and insincere apologies is that the person who makes them may become terribly hurt if they are greeted somewhat half-heartedly. Again, the first thing you should do is take control of the situation by controlling your own reaction. You should be careful not to respond in any of the following ways:

- 'I'll give you the benefit of the doubt.'
- 'It really sounds like it wasn't your fault.'
- 'Maybe if I overlook it this time he will improve.'
- 'Alright, because you apologised, I will forget about it.'

All of the above are fine under normal circumstances but not when you are dealing with a child who constantly puts the blame somewhere else, who always has an excuse, and does this to the extent that her chances of becoming a responsible adult are endangered. As far as possible, she should know what the consequences of her behaviour *will* be so that arguments about what the consequences *should* be are avoided. (A great deal more will be said about this in the chapter 8, 'Consequences'.)

Once you have controlled your own reaction to the efforts of your child to deny blame, you will be able to give some thought to the probable cause of the problem. The most common cause is that you have been so concerned for the welfare of your child that, from long habit, you have continued to rescue him from consequences long after he has grown old enough to be allowed to experience them. You have no doubt acted out of love for your child but now would probably experience far fewer problems if you learnt to express that love in a different way.

There is, however, a very serious side to a child's feelings of inadequacy. It is a fair bet that a child who constantly lays the blame elsewhere feels very discouraged, as well as useless and worthless. In short, she feels she has little control over what happens in her life. Everything seems to be decided and controlled by other people; she cannot feel responsible for anything that goes right or wrong because she has no real say.

This lack of control can result in two very different attitudes:

1 'It doesn't matter what I do, I have no say in it, so I can't be blamed.'
2 'Nothing I do will matter so what's the use of trying?'

The first of these attitudes will allow the child to do anything while passing the blame on to something or someone else. It may result in self-destructive behaviour like unsafe sex, drugs, alcohol abuse and law-breaking. The second will allow the child to avoid doing anything much about meeting his own needs. He may become withdrawn, avoid all eye contact and have no opinion about anything. He may even start to deliberately inflict pain or punishment on himself.

No matter which of these attitudes is displayed, the feeling behind it is one of being helpless and worthless. In some cases this feeling may become quite desperate and, if a child believes it will not pass, it may well lead to depression or even suicide. Whatever you do, *do not underestimate the depth of this feeling*. If you are concerned about this possibility, seek professional help through your local community services.

Summary

All human behaviour has a purpose and this includes misbehaviour. Through years of experience, starting at birth, children learn how to act to get a desired response from their parents. However, parents can learn to recognise the purpose of the behaviour, to work out what is going wrong in the relationship, and to take charge of their parenting situation.

This can be done by noting what feelings are stirred up by the behaviour. Is it power, attention, revenge or inadequacy? Once this becomes clear the situation can be dealt with by reacting in an unexpected way. The reaction may be to back away from a power struggle, to control the attention given and ignore demanded attention, to resist the urge to get even, or to encourage teenagers to take control of their own lives.

CHANGING THE PARENT–CHILD RELATIONSHIP

What you can change

It's a fairly sure bet that, if you are a parent reading this book, you are having trouble maintaining control of a family situation that involves young people. It is also a fairly sure bet that you realise that something has to change. Like so many other parents, you probably feel that no matter what you do, nothing seems to make any difference. You try and try to change the way your children act but all to no avail, and your relationship with them may be getting steadily worse. This is not the way you want it to be, you would rather have a good relationship with your kids and for them to be able to come to you with their problems.

There *are* ways, as I have stressed, that you can have more control of your situation and bring about change. But first of all you need to be aware of what can be changed and what cannot. Second, you must know what it is *possible* for you to change and what is *not possible* for you to change. Most things in this world change, but not all things that can change can be changed by *you*. The way you act, however, can have a great effect on those things that can change. For instance, what you decide to do can influence what all the people around you decide to do. And you can develop this influence to a point where you feel you have control of a situation — it takes practice but you can do it.

The effect of the past on the present

Of all the things that cannot be changed, the past is by far the biggest. The past includes everything that has ever happened, even what happened only a moment ago is in the past and cannot be changed. You may do something to make up for a past action but there is no way to alter the fact that it happened. No amount of worrying will alter one fraction of the past, so any time spent worrying about the past is well and truly wasted. If you read the previous paragraph, it is now a fact that you read it and nothing you do in the future can ever change that. You may decide not to read any more of this book but you cannot undo the reading you have done so far.

Included in the past is everything that has ever happened to you:

- Where you were born;
- The nationality of your parents;
- Your family background;
- How you have been treated by others;
- Who you have loved and who you have disliked;
- How many children you have had and with whom;
- How you have treated your children and how they have treated you;
- How you have acted in the past;
- How you acted a moment ago.

The sorts of problems that are in your past may include things like:

- You may have divorced and remarried. Nothing can alter that and nothing can alter the way your children reacted to it.
- If you were born into a strict religious family and believe you were 'brainwashed' into thinking certain things, there is nothing you can do about it. This was the case and all the things you have done were affected by it.
- If you have diabetes, you have to accept this and allow for it when you make decisions.
- If your children appear to be rebelling against your authority over them, you would be better off accepting that that is the way it is at the moment, and it is due to something in the past that cannot be changed.

Another thing you cannot change is another person's way of doing things. It is virtually impossible to force another person to do something she does not want to do. Even if you threaten her, she can still say 'no'. Offering rewards may also be used as a way of getting someone to do something — nevertheless, that person is still free to say 'no'. So you can make the rewards very attractive or the threats very daunting, but a person can still refuse to go along with you. In the end you must accept that while you can *influence* a person to change you cannot *make* him change. A person only changes when he *wants* to.

The effect of the present on the future

I believe that all of the above can be put into a few words: 'Accept the present situation and do the best you can with it'. The golden rule here is to concentrate on controlling what you do *now*, without worrying about how you have performed in the past. 'What can I do *now* to work towards what I want?'

You cannot alter the past that led to the present and you

cannot make other people, including your children, change their behaviour. However, what you decide to do now will greatly influence the future by influencing the way your kids act, simply because their decisions have to take your actions into account. This point is so important that I am going to discuss it at some length.

Unfortunately, too many of our actions are actually habits, which we come to feel we can't really change. But making decisions about the way we act gives us some control over our lives and what happens in the future. The more often we *choose* how we are going to act, the more control we have over ourselves and the more control we have over how we can influence other people.

Although we do not treat every person we know in the same way, we do seem to get into the habit of relating in a particular way to each individual. For example, you undoubtedly treat your best friend in a different way to the way you treat the two year old from next door, even though it is possible for you to treat them both the same way, simply because you have that choice. Indeed, it is even possible for you to reverse the way you treat your best friend and the two year old from next door.

Too many people, at all ages, seem to believe that the future is decided by the past. They may use this thinking as an excuse for not trying or as a reason for their failures. This is all too true when it comes to using things from the past to explain the way we act. Because adults do this so much, so do children. Children can become quite expert at it, blaming all sorts of things for their behaviour and leaving their parents feeling that they are to blame for nearly everything. Sometimes a child takes advantage of the fact that his parents feel guilty about something that happened a long time ago; they may be willing, for example, to give him anything he wants to make up for it.

We should not accept that our future is controlled by our past, that we have no say in what happens to us. Likewise, we should not accept that we must act in the same ways we have always acted. It is worth repeating the fact that you cannot alter the past that led to the present but what you do now may greatly influence the future. What you decide to do in response to your child's behaviour will greatly influence what your child decides to do. Just because things have not gone well between you in the past does not mean that things have to go badly in the future.

Just for a moment, try to imagine what would happen if you decided to treat your best friend in the same way that you treat the two year old from next door. It is not too much to suggest that your friend's actions towards you would also change. Spend a few minutes imagining what would happen if you reversed the way you normally treat these people. How do you imagine each would react? The point is that each would react differently towards you than they normally do, simply because you decided to alter the way you acted towards them.

Unfortunately, it is very difficult to change the way we treat a particular person, because of the habits we have got into. It is particularly difficult to change our reactions to a child's behaviour and it takes a conscious effort to do so, especially when we are upset. It is true that people do not *make* us angry, that we allow ourselves to get angry even though we could avoid this by acting differently. For example, we could think about how we handled a certain situation last time it came up, think about what went wrong, and decide on a better course of action for next time. When the situation crops up again we can try out our plan to see if things improve. All this may require some practice and each time we try to alter a situation we should ask ourselves how it improved and what parts still need working on. This is positive thinking. The problem may not be solved immediately but, if we are willing to learn from our mistakes, and try again or try another way, at least we are moving forward.

How to decide whose problem it is

Another practical way of dealing with a problem situation is to decide who really should be dealing with it, just whose problem it really is. There are two questions that will help you decide this fairly quickly:

1 Who made the approach about it?
2 Do I want (to) help?

For the moment I will discuss only the first question. I will come back to the second question later in the chapter. Whoever receives the nod to the first question is the owner of the problem and is the one who is responsible for solving it. This is a simple statement about a simple question, and can help remove a great deal of the frustration you feel and lessen the number of conflicts between you and your offspring. It means that if your child approaches you it is his problem, and so he is responsible for finding a solution. On the other hand, if you approach your child then it is your problem and you are responsible for solving it.

When it is your child's problem

Some examples may make the above point clearer. A child wanders around the house, among all sorts of playthings you have worked hard to provide, and says, 'I'm bored. What is there to do around this dump?'. Remember the first question: 'Who made the approach?' Answer: the child. So you can assume that it is the child who has the problem, not you. She is trying to make it your problem and is usually quite good at getting you to accept responsibility for providing some kind of entertainment. If you accept her problem as your own you will probably become increasingly frustrated as everything you suggest gets knocked back by a child who is busily thinking up all sorts of reasons why your suggestions are no good — 'It's too hard', 'It's too easy', 'It's too hot', 'It's too cold', 'There's no-one to go with', 'He's sick of that', 'That's a dumb suggestion', or 'That's all you ever say'.

This may be a well-worn track that seems to get nowhere, and to produce nothing except irritation. But the real reason for this is that you are trying to solve a problem that is not your own. The child is the owner of the problem and she is the one who should be trying to solve it, not you. Looking at it another way, the child has managed to solve her problem by

getting you to play a game that she has found she can suck you into every time. She is no longer bored — this is good fun!

If it isn't a game then you have been tricked into allowing the child to dump his problem on to you while he gets out of the responsibility of solving it and learning a little about independence.

When the child is the one who owns the problem, let her know this by using the word, 'you':

- 'You are bored. Well, what are you going to do about it?'
- 'What do you usually do about it when you are bored?'
- 'What did you do the last time you were bored?'
- 'What do your friends do when they get bored?'

It doesn't matter how you put it as long as the word 'you' is used to let him know that it is his problem to solve. In doing this you have taken advantage of an opportunity to encourage him to make decisions about his own life.

Example one: A teenager comes storming out of her room, yelling at all and sundry, and demanding to know from her mother where her best pair of jeans are and why they are not in her drawer. Who made the approach? Quite obviously, the teenager. Now her mother could do what she normally does, which is to become very apologetic and run around looking for the jeans and then put off everything else to iron them. But she could say to herself, 'Hey, hang on a minute, whose problem is this?' Her daughter owns the problem and this can be put to her by saying something like:

- 'You can't find your jeans. Let me know if you can't find them after you have looked in all the likely places.'
- 'You need those jeans for tonight so where do you think they might be?'
- 'You certainly sound angry with yourself for not knowing where those jeans are.'

Example two: A child tells his father he wants a bike. The child made the approach so it is the child's problem. Dad is a wake-up by now, and after thinking about who made the approach, he says something like:

- 'How are you going to pay for it?'
- 'What are you going to do about it?'
- 'How are you going to help get the money for it?'

As I said before, the important thing is that a child becomes aware that she is capable of solving her own problems, and so learns something about being an independent and responsible person.

When it is your problem

An example here would be when your teenage son comes home and tracks mud through the house, drops his clothes, books and schoolbag on the floor of the lounge room that you have just tidied up and plonks himself down to watch television. You track him down and angrily tell him what you think about this, and demand that he wipe his shoes in future, that he pick up his gear now and put it away where it should be.

But wait! Whose problem is it? Who made the approach? You did. So, in this case, you are the one who really owns the problem, because you approached the boy about the mess. He made the mess and you are upset by it. The only problem your son has is that he is confronted with an angry parent, and he has to decide how to react. The messy lounge room floor doesn't worry him one little bit, in fact it probably goes quite well with his bedroom.

It is very hard to maintain control of a situation when you are angry, and the more angry you become, the more the situation can move out of your control. Being confident in knowing who is responsible for solving problems will help you to control situations like the one above. I would suggest that you do this by asking yourself 'Whose problem is this?' before approaching your child, because this will help you keep calm. The mere fact that you have stopped long enough to ask that question means that you have practised considerable self-control. If you can do this it will help you avoid approaching the problem in the wrong way. It may well be true that you have been 'wronged' in some way, but because you are the one who is making the approach you are the owner of the problem.

Sometimes a child will show some understanding of all this. For instance, in the above example, the teenage boy may be confronted by an angry parent who claims he is a lazy, ungrateful, sloppy misfit who never does anything around the house except make a mess. He calmly looks up from the television and says, 'If you want the lounge tidy, you clean it up. It's your problem, not mine'. This can make you even angrier and can lead to a full-blown power struggle that must end in someone, usually you, losing.

When you are the one making the approach, acknowledge that you are aware that it is your problem, by using the word 'I':

- 'I am upset about the mud on the floor from your shoes and about the stuff you left on the floor of the lounge, especially after all my effort to tidy up the house today. I would be happier if you put things right by cleaning up the mud and putting your gear away.'
- 'I spent a lot of time cleaning the house today so I could relax tonight. I would appreciate it if you could clean up

the mud from your shoes and put away the gear you left on the lounge floor.'
- 'I want the house to be clean and tidy tonight, as it was before you came home. Now it will have to be done again.'

The important thing is to let it be known that you are aware that you own the problem, even though in this case you are trying to get co-operation from your son. The use of the word 'I' lets the lad know that you realise the problem is yours, and he is more likely to co-operate if you say this.

The above suggestions put a lot of pressure on your son to put things right, but of course things are not always this simple. For instance, the child may reply, 'So, who cares what you think? Do it yourself!'. While this sort of response is possible it is not likely unless the relationship is bad. If something along these lines was said, however, whatever you decide to do would need to be something you have full control over. Perhaps you would tell him what you intend to do about it and when. Then, without saying anything further, you might pick up the gear and put it away, maybe somewhere that takes some effort for your son to get it next time he wants it.

Like a great many parents, you probably find it fairly difficult to approach your teenage children about a problem without ending up in an argument, even when you are only wanting to show concern. The conversation hardly gets going, it seems, before your daughter becomes defensive and doesn't want to talk about it, or will just blindly argue against you. If this happens, it is highly likely that you have used the word 'you' to set down who owns the problem, when it should have been 'I', because you made the approach. The word 'you' is a very accusing word, and a very attacking word. Young people are quick to put up defences against attack, especially when they believe they are being wrongly accused. Approaching someone about a problem and using the word 'you' is wrongly accusing that person of owning the problem and, looking at it this way, it is understandable that he becomes defensive.

When you wish to approach a young person about a problem, it may be difficult to work out *why* it is your problem and how to present it thus. The general guide here is that you are probably concerned about some kind of harm coming to the young person. All you need to work out is what you are afraid might happen, and say this in your opening remark:

- 'I am concerned that if you ride your bike without lights you will get hurt and I don't want that to happen.'
- 'I am afraid that you are going to get into trouble if you keep knocking about with your new friend.'
- 'I am deeply anxious that you will fail your exam and would feel much happier if I could have a look at your study plan.'
- 'I find it very difficult to understand the attitude of young people towards sex.'
- 'I constantly worry about you walking home after dark.'
- 'I am afraid that you will get badly hurt if you don't wear a helmet.'
- 'I have always believed that abortion is wrong and must oppose what you intend doing.'
- 'I get frustrated and angry when you mess up the lounge room.'

All of the above statements squarely place the problem as belonging to the speaker. No accusation is evident and each one invites discussion, between equals, to try to find a solution to a problem.

Sharing a problem

'But I want to share my child's problem and help solve it.' If asked whether they wanted to share their children's problems, most parents would answer 'yes'. Parents are parents and they want to help their kids. After all, they have been doing this ever since the children were born, and it gives them great satisfaction to be able to express their love by helping them through their troubles.

Back at the beginning of this discussion on who owns a problem, I mentioned two questions and have considered only one of them so far. Now it is time to talk about the other question, which is, 'Do I want (to) help?' We can see that the first question must be answered before the second one can be asked, because the answer to the first question shapes the second one.

I have put brackets around the word (to) because the question can be asked in two ways depending on who is responsible for solving the problem. If the answer to the first question is 'the child', the second question becomes, 'Do I want to help?'. If the answer to the first question is 'me', then the second question is, 'Do I want help?'. And of course the desire to share problem-solving introduces the use of the word 'we'.

Once it is decided who owns the problem and that it should be a shared problem, the word 'we' can be used to either offer help, or appeal for help. We can use the example of the bored child again here. Suppose you have decided that you want to help the child out. There are several different levels of help that can be offered. Read through the following alternatives:

- 'You are bored. Well, what do you think we can do about it?' This reply goes part way by offering to join in an activity.
- 'How do you usually solve this problem? Maybe we can think of some new ways.' This reply offers to join in the thinking part of solving the problem but not necessarily the doing part.
- 'You tell me some of the ways you have got over boredom in the past and I may be able to make other suggestions.' The word 'we' is not actually mentioned in this reply but it is implied by the offer of help, once again without taking responsibility away from the child.

Whatever actual reply you choose, you can still let the child know who really owns the problem by using 'you', then bringing in the word 'we' (or combining 'you' and 'I' to imply 'we') to show that you are willing to help with this problem. Similar responses are applicable where the boy wants a bike:

- 'You want a bike and you need the money to get one. What do you think we can do to get what you want?'
- 'You tell me the ways you have thought of to get the money to buy the bike, and maybe we can work out how to go about it.'
- 'You want a bike but you don't have enough money to buy one. Maybe we can work out a way that you can earn some extra money.'
- 'You want a bike. I want to help, so tell me how you think I can help and I'll tell you if it's ok.'

Where the problem belongs to you, you should be aware of this before making the approach so that the wording you use puts responsibility where it belongs, and asks for co-operation. This means that before approaching a child with your problem, you should be clear on just what your problem is. For an example here, let's return to the messy teenage son:

- 'I want to have the lounge tidy again but I need your help. Can we talk about it?'
- 'I tidied up the house today and now it looks worse than when I started. I really need your help in this, so we can have a clean house.'
- 'I want the house to be clean and tidy most of the time, and I'm sure that we can work out a way for it to stay tidy, at least for a while after I've tidied up.'

How to reduce the range of problem areas

There are enough problems to deal with between parents and children without also having other individuals and groups cause trouble between you. Parents and children can fight about problems presented by outsiders when those problems really belong to the third party. Fortunately, the method of deciding who is really responsible for solving problems presented here can be used in any situation, not only between parents and their children. It can be used to eliminate many of the problems presented from outside the parent–child relationship. For instance, a school can cause you a great deal of frustration by trying to palm off its own problems on you. The school may make a rule and then expect parents to enforce it, or it may have a discipline problem and be trying to get you to 'do something about young Johnny's attitude'.

This sort of demand is the cause of many conflicts between parents and children, and again frustration results because you are being asked to solve a problem that is not your own. For example, the school sends a note home to say that Mary's behaviour towards the teachers is disgraceful and that you are 'requested' to do something about this. Or perhaps your son is caught smoking at school and is suspended until you come to the school for a meeting with the principal. Up till now you probably felt like a failure as a parent, and so you dutifully go to meet the principal and apologise profusely for the behaviour of your child. Now, however, with your knowledge that it is the school that owns the problem, you can go to the meeting willing to support the school if they can find a solution. This is an entirely different way of handling a situation in which a third party is involved.

Many occasions arise when the problem being presented from outside the family is a problem that you want to share. When the school principal sends a note home about your son's behaviour at school, your note in reply could read something like, 'Your school system does seem to have a problem that we may be able to solve between us. I would be quite happy to offer you some advice on this matter'.

I believe this example really shows up the advantage of knowing who actually has the responsibility for solving a problem. Your knowledge of who is responsible will allow you to meet the principal as someone she has called on for help, rather than as someone who has to apologise for having raised a brat. First, you have let the principal know that it is her problem and, second, that you are willing to share it, without actually taking the responsibility of solving it. You are the expert she has called on for help because of your vast knowledge of your son. The same rules about the use of 'I', 'you', and 'we' apply when dealing with your children, school principals, or anyone else.

Solving the problem

So far we have talked about who is responsible for solving a problem, and whether a problem should be shared, but how do you actually go about solving it? The first thing is to avoid open warfare, as in those situations of utter frustration in which a teenager seems to swing quite comfortably between logic and using any sort of ridiculous information just to win a point. Teenagers can be very competitive once they get locked into an argument, so that winning becomes more important than either truth or justice. This can even apply when they are arguing about the importance of truth or justice.

But this need to win is very strong in all of us. Where there is a conflict of needs, one or other of the people involved will lose. One of the real problems with constantly using the win or lose approach is that the odds are in favour of the most powerful, and if this power is always in the hands of one, the other may become extremely resentful. Although the more powerful person wins the immediate tussle, it will probably lead to resentment, and resentment leads to revenge.

The actual power struggle is taking place when you and the child are struggling over who is going to win and who is going to lose. The resentment comes when there is a winner and a loser. In a prolonged power struggle, resentment seems to fill the gap between battles.

In the past, when your child was smaller and there was a conflict of needs, he would usually have backed down in the end, because you were seen as being wiser and/or bigger. As far as the small child is concerned, his parents are nearly always right and if they are not right then they are bigger, and besides, they have control over the good things in life. However, since the child has reached adolescence, and no longer sees you as being always right, or as being the biggest, or as having control over the good things of life, the one to lose has probably been you. But this is not necessary. The idea that one person must back down implies that there are only two possible solutions — either you win or you lose.

I don't see anything wrong in 'backing off' from a bad situation to allow time for you or your child, or both of you, to cool down. Backing off is often the most sensible way to handle a power struggle situation, and you can do this very easily by saying something like:

- 'I still intend to talk this out but I think we should leave it until we both cool down.'
- 'I want to talk to you about this, but I am too upset at the moment and might say something I don't really mean.'
- 'It is quite obvious that we are not going to find a solution while we are angry, so I will approach you again once things have cooled down.'
- 'I don't think we are really ready to discuss this yet. Let me know when you are ready to find a solution.'

How both of you can be winners

There is a better way to handle conflicts between you and your child, a way that doesn't involve winning or losing. You may be able to find a solution that suits both of you, because both your needs have been considered. The solution to any parent–child conflict must involve a change in one or more of the following:

1 You must change in some way;
2 Your child must change in some way;
3 Something in the environment common to both of you must change in some way.

This means that any problem between you and your child can only be solved by a change in one or a combination of these three things. It could be how often you see each other, how you act towards each other, whether you part company for a while, or whether you stop living in the same house altogether. The latter may also entail a change in the problem-solving relationship between you and your child. The first two ways are the old win/lose solutions which we are so familiar with that I will not discuss them.

The third alternative, changing something in the environment, may be much harder for you to do than for your child. Perhaps this is because you believe it is your duty to do all you can for your child, that you may lose her love if you don't keep doing all the things you have always done. There may be many good reasons why you have solved problems for your child in the past, but at adolescence she may be crying out for the right to solve them for herself. On the other hand, she may go to great lengths to avoid taking responsiblity for her problems, even if she is well old enough. No matter what the reason, this third and most effective method of problem-solving is the most difficult to get people to try out. Given that it generally involves a change in the problem-solving relationship, it is somewhat surprising that people can be so reluctant to use it.

As I said, the best solutions are those that allow for the needs of both you and your child. These solutions go something like, 'I realise that your needs are just as important to you as mine are to me'. I am talking about communication and trust, not a wishy-washy sort of compromise which really amounts to, 'I'll let you win this one if you let me win the next one'. I am talking about assertiveness in a healthy relationship, in which the needs of both parties are recognised and respected.

It is not so easy to find brief examples to demonstrate this method of problem-solving, because it involves each person helping to find a satisfactory solution. However, here are some statements which may set the stage for discussions around the needs of each person, or which immediately offer a solution that takes account of the needs of each:

- After your television show is finished I want to talk to you about a problem I have.'
- 'I want the house to be tidy and you want to watch television but you've made the house untidy by leaving your gear lying around. Could you please put it away during the next break?'
- 'I feel unhappy that we don't seem to be getting on very well lately. Can we talk about this?'
- 'I get worried and upset about you walking home after

dark but I know you don't want me to pick you up. What if I give you the taxi fare each time you're going to be late?'

- 'I am afraid that people at parties are going to slip you drugs without you knowing. Can we talk about the ways you can avoid this, so I'll feel a bit less concerned about it?'
- 'I'm worried that you are growing up in a society in which AIDS is a problem. How about bringing some information home from school so I know what you are learning about it?'
- 'I want to listen to some of my music at times. Can we come to some arrangement on this?'
- 'I worry about the friends you knock about with because I know they are doing things that I think will cause you trouble if you start doing the same. I realise that you have the right to pick your own friends, and I respect that right, but I don't have to approve of all your friends, just as you don't have to approve of all mine. I can't stop you from seeing them, but I will not do anything to encourage it.'

I have found that a statement like the last one, about friends you do not approve of, may prompt a child to rethink the situation himself. This is certainly much more positve than spending hours arguing about the good and bad points of his friends. It may be necessary to state once what you are unhappy about, but it would be unwise to get into an argument about it. You should listen to your son's reply to what you are saying, but if that doesn't change your opinion, you should simply repeat that you will do nothing to encourage the friendships although you realise that you cannot stop them.

Summary

When a relationship is going badly, something has to change, but the only thing that any of us can really change is ourselves. We cannot change the past and we cannot change another person. What we do in the present can influence what happens in the future and what others do but other people only change if they want to.

One way we can reduce conflict is to work out who is responsible for solving the problem. This is done by asking two questions: 'Who approached who?' and, 'Do I want (to) help?' and then using 'I', 'you' and 'we' to let ourselves and others know who owns the problem and who is responsible for solving it. Solving shared problems works better if the old win/lose method is replaced with the win/win method which takes both parties' needs into account.

CHAPTER 4

BEING ASSERTIVE WITH TEENAGERS

Mutual respect

The best and most rewarding relationships are assertive relationships. In assertive relationships each person respects the rights of the other; the two are therefore on equal footing. The best and most rewarding parent–child relationships are also assertive relationships. But many people make the mistake of thinking that statements like these mean that the parent and child have equal responsibilities and privileges. This is not so, what is really meant is that you and your child have equal rights as people, even though you have different responsibilities towards each other and towards other people. Indeed, it is quite obvious that you have different responsibilities and privileges to your child, and that you have the authority to carry out those responsibilities.

Although they differ, your child's responsibilities and problems are just as important to her as yours are to you, and her way of solving her problems is just as precious to her as your way of solving your problems is to you.

Your greatest responsibility as a parent is to help your child develop into an independent adult. This is something you started doing as soon as the child was born. Now, as an adolescent, the child is almost through his training period and is probably very impatient to have a go at flying solo. He is almost ready for this adventure, but not quite. Every child can be thought of as an apprentice adult and the adolescent child can be thought of as being very nearly through that apprenticeship. You have passed on many of the skills he needs to do a good job of being an adult, and the time is now very near when he will be on his own.

During this period many problems arise that you, as a parent, feel a responsibility to deal with. This is fine, but you must be sure that you deal with them in a way that encourages your child to take more and more responsibility for her own behaviour. We will talk more about this aspect of parenting in the final chapter. For now I want to go into a bit more detail about assertiveness.

We have already talked about a way to work out, and state, who is responsible for finding a solution to a problem. We have also looked at ways of sharing problems. You might argue that in doing all that we have covered the topic of 'assertiveness'. Indeed, we have covered a lot to do with assertiveness, but there is still another important point we should look at. To be assertive means to stick up for yourself, to say what you think and to carry out your responsibilities. It also means to respect the rights and responsibilities of others in the same way that you expect your rights to be respected. Respecting another's rights is easy enough when everything is going well, but when you are not happy about what somebody has done, it can be very difficult to avoid criticising and insulting her. In this chapter I will suggest ways of maintaining your respect for others while criticising their behaviour.

There are all sorts of ways that another person's behaviour can cause you problems, but here I want to concentrate on problems you might want to talk to your child about. As adults, we often don't seem to think very much before we criticise kids, yet we are very cautious about criticising other adults, at least to their faces. What makes it even easier to criticise kids is that in general they seem to accept that adults have the right to criticise them. Adolescent kids, however, are super-sensitive to criticism and so parents should be at least as thoughtful in criticising them as they are in criticising other adults. Kids are people too, so the suggestions made here apply no matter whose behaviour you want to criticise.

When criticising, whose problem is it?

We immediately run into a problem when we decide to criticise someone because, as you will remember from the previous chapter, the fact that you are the one who wants to bring up the problem means that you are the one who owns it. And you must approach it that way, that is, you must acknowledge that you own the problem by using the word 'I' when you approach the child.

Now you may well ask how what someone else does can suddenly be turned around to become your problem. The simple answer is that the fault does not become yours, but what you see as someone else's fault is causing you a problem. For this reason it would be better to replace the word 'criticise' with 'feedback', in other words to change from criticising the other person to giving feedback on what effect their actions are having on you.

The problems you may wish to talk to your child about will probably include:

- Problems that have affected you and you are able to explain how quite easily;
- Problems that have affected others and you are able to explain how quite easily;
- Problems that you are concerned may cause harm to the child's relationships with other people;
- Problems that you fear may cause some harm to the child if her behaviour doesn't change.
- Problems that you cannot prove have any definite effect on you or others, as in the case of value differences.

These three examples demonstrate that people have needs that they believe can be best satisfied in certain ways, and they place great value on the things that satisfy them. Their behaviour will be the result of what they believe is the best way to satisfy their needs, and is the expression of their beliefs and values. All this goes to make up what we refer to as someone's *attitude*.

What are values?

Many of the things you will want to discuss with your child will concern value differences. Value differences can cause many relationship problems between parents and adolescents so you must tread very carefully. Believe me, if you are going to talk to an adolescent about anything at all, you are far better off if you understand exactly what you are talking about. So what does the word 'values' mean? It is helpful to look at the word in relation to some other very common words which are not easily explained. These include 'needs', 'beliefs', 'behaviour' and 'attitude'. Look at the following three examples:

Example one: Father has a *need* to be healthy. He *believes* that a balanced diet will go a long way to satisfy that need so he places great *value* on fresh vegetables and certain recipes. He spends a lot of time *looking after* his garden and keeping his recipes in order. Most people agree that he has a good *attitude* to health.

Example two: Mother has a *need* to serve God. She *believes* that to serve God she must serve other people. She places great *value* on helping people less fortunate than herself and tries hard to aid them in any way she can. People who know her say she has a wonderful *attitude* towards the poor and homeless.

Example three: I am out of work. I am broke and need food.
I *believe* that money will satisfy my need. I also *believe* in the
survival of the fittest and in looking after Number One, and
that's why I steal and cheat to get money. People reckon my
attitude stinks, but I don't really care what they think.

Because a person's behaviour expresses their beliefs and
values, we tend to judge their attitudes from their behaviour
without taking into account their needs. If we take needs into
account then the attitude of the person in the third example is
more easily understood.

The teenager's confused value system

Mature adults know from experience that certain relationships and things will help them satisfy their needs, and so
these relationships and things become part of their value

system. Adolescents, however, are still trying to find out what will satisfy their needs, and so what relationships and things will be valuable to them. To put it another way, they are searching for their own set of values to meet their own set of needs. Because they don't have an established way of satisfying their needs, they may value different things at different times. Adolescents who have not established a value system appear to grab at whatever is available in each situation to satisfy their immediate needs, and this helps explain why they may 'throw it all away' for an immediate gain.

Usually this doesn't cause much of a problem, and the kids will learn from experience. It becomes a major problem, however, when it involves the consequences of unsafe sex and other life-threatening activities. Some kids even value indulging in life-threatening activities, and no amount of talking will deter them. They may need to feel the kind of 'high' that goes with dangerous activities, like bungee jumping or drugs. To most of us this may appear rather stupid but remember there are plenty of adults who do bungee jumping and/or take drugs.

Each of us has a unique set of needs and each of us values the things that help us to satisfy those needs. The adolescent needs to find out what things will satisfy her needs, and most of her values will be the same as those of her peers. Because adolescents are still experimenting to find out what they value, though, they may confuse the value they place on things. What they value today may be worthless to them tomorrow. An adolescent girl may be ready to die for a particular boy today, and intensely hate the same boy tomorrow. An adolescent may work hard to earn enough money to buy a particular pair of jeans, and then cut holes in them because his favourite pop singer appeared on stage that way.

Despite the fact that people have different needs and different ways of satisfying those needs, many values are common to all people, whatever their age. It is assumed here that set laws are made because most people agree on the values they are intended to enforce. Therefore, values that are covered by set laws *cannot* be regarded as 'value differences'.

There is one other point which is important here, because it helps explain why some people break laws and rules they claim to agree with. To make this clearer imagine three people who each say that they value the law as a guide to how they should behave, and yet have very different attitudes to staying within the law.

First person's attitude: I value the law as a guide because it tells me what I can get away with and what I can't get away with. I can bend the law and even break it because there isn't much chance of getting caught, and even if I do get caught they have to prove that I did it.

Second person's attitude: I value the law as a guide because accepted values keep changing. Something that most people accept as 'right' today may have been 'wrong' yesterday, or vice versa. If I keep to the law, regardless of what the law is, I am doing the right thing.

Third person's attitude: I value the law as a guide but some of my values are my own, and they do not change as the law changes. I believe that those values are universal values and are above the law. If the law clashes with those values, I will act according to my values.

These examples help to show that even when you and your child agree that something is valuable, you may still interpret that value differently. These different meanings can cause bitter conflicts between you, even though you both agree that these things are valuable in meeting your needs.

There are many values the law does not deal with because whether or not you have those values does not (normally) affect others in any way, and whether or not others have those values does not (normally) affect you in any way. Values that have little or no affect on others are the values I mean when I talk about 'value differences'. Some examples include:

- The length of my hair;
- The clothes I wear;
- How often I have a shower;
- How tidy I keep my room;
- What colours I wear together;
- Who I like and who I dislike;

- Whether I smoke and/or drink and how much;
- Whether I play sport or whether I prefer to watch;
- Whether I eat meat or not;
- Who I have sex with;
- How much sleep I want;
- How clean my shoes are;
- Whether I go to church or not;
- Who I have as my friends.

Of course the list could go on and on. It can include all those things that you and I, and everyone else, have the freedom to chose to do or not to do, according to how they help us satisfy some desire or need.

Where do values come from?

Values are handed on by example, so children learn their values by observing how those values work for other people. The value you place on something shows up in the way you act towards that thing, rather than from what you say about it. This is why values are passed on by example rather than from lectures. When it comes to values, the old saying 'Don't do as I do, do as I say' is just so much hot air. Children learn their values by seeing how they work for you — how you act towards a particular thing, not from what you say about it.

Very young children live according to the values held by their parents and other people who are important to them, like relatives and teachers, and they may not question these values at all. However, at adolescence they set about comparing those values with the values of others, so they can form their own set of values. The most likely outcome is that the child will eventually form a set of values that are much the same as those of his parents, even though most of the conflicts they had in the past were over value differences.

And parents are quite likely to have unwittingly passed on values that they would say they do not agree with. For instance, if there was a difference between what you said and what you did at the time your child was taking notice, it is your *actions* that she would have taken count of. This is because although words may reflect what you think your values should be, your actions reflect what your real values are. You might believe, for example, that you have always taught your child that 'honesty is the best policy', but your child may have seen your words and actions in a very different way.

Example one: Someone you don't want to talk to phones up, so you tell the person who answers the phone to tell the caller that you are not home.

Example two: You want to go to the tennis on a working day, so you get your wife to phone work and tell the boss you are sick.

You may claim that such actions are just 'little white lies', but your child might see them as, 'Lying is ok if it gets you what you want'. Furthermore, he may become confused when he tries it himself as a way out of trouble but then cops a punishment for lying. This might teach him that 'Lying is ok, but only for adults'.

Another way you may unwittingly allow values that are different to your own to be passed onto your children is through television. You may once have believed that television viewing would not harm your children, but now you may be questioning this. If this is the case, then remember that the values shown on television may have been watched more than what your values were, so now you have the job of correcting any harm done. Values may also be learnt from other relatives, other adults, other kids, and teachers; there is very little sense in blaming yourself if your child has a value which you disapprove of.

Adolescence is the time to correct the values you have unwittingly passed on to your child, but this will not happen by fighting about them. Correcting a value is much more likely to occur if you state *once* what your true value is and then show, through your actions, that this satisfies your needs. It is through seeing values working for you that your child will take notice of them.

How to criticise teenagers' behaviour

There are four rules to remember when you have a problem you want to discuss with your child. They are the same rules that apply when approaching an adult about a problem, and we can refer to them as the Rules of Feedback. They are:

1   Give the child all the information necessary about the problem without demanding any correction;
2   Separate the child from the behaviour;
3   Stick to one problem;
4   Be positive and give encouragement.

Give all the information necessary about the problem without demanding any correction

When your child is very young, there are many times when you have to work out the solution to a problem, and many times when it is necessary for your child to follow instructions without being told why. This may be because there isn't time to explain the reason, or it may be that your child would not be able to understand the reasons behind the instructions. These are times when 'Because I said so' is probably reason enough.

However, as your child matures and moves closer to having to work out most problems for herself, 'Because I said so' becomes less and less acceptable from you. If she doesn't know what the problem is, how can she be expected to do anything about it? Like most of us, you may have fallen into the habit of saying things that really don't help your child to know what you are upset about. Sentences like the following are commonly used but are not very helpful:

- 'Your attitude stinks.'
- 'You give me a pain in the neck.'
- 'When are you ever going to grow up?'
- 'For goodness sake, wake up to yourself.'

These sentences do nothing to help solve the problem because they give no information as to what is causing it. The child is given no idea what he can do to change the situation, even if he wanted to.

There are many different ways of getting information across to a child, but a simple one to practise is the 'I feel . . . when . . . because . . .'. method. To do this effectively though, you must know exactly how the problem is affecting you and your feelings. Some examples are:

- 'I feel angry when you make so much noise at night because I can't sleep.'
- 'I felt very hurt when you didn't pay back that money I lent you because I told you I needed it to pay the phone bill.'

The 'I . . . feel . . . when . . . because . . .' method gives all the information a child needs to know: *how* you are being affected, *what* part of her behaviour affects you and the *reason* why it affects you.

One advantage of using this method is that you are making no demand whatsoever for the behaviour to be changed. You have made a simple statement about how you are affected by a certain behaviour and why you are affected in this way. Whether or not a child changes his behaviour is entirely up to him, but at least he knows how the behaviour is being received and why you are angry, hurt, or annoyed.

By not demanding that a child's behaviour change you actually allow for a change to occur, because a child needs approval. Whenever you demand a change you risk causing an argument, as the child tries to defend against what she sees as an attack on her way of doing things. Children are no different to other people, they all want approval and to get along with others, so they will usually change a behaviour if someone disapproves of it. Therefore, most of the time, it is only necessary to let a child know what behaviour is disapproved of.

Some children still become defensive when the 'I feel . . . when . . . because . . .' method is used and, when this happens, you can say something like, 'Well, I'm only telling you how that behaviour affects me and why it affects me that way. It's up to you to decide whether or not you keep it up, but it's up to me to decide whether I stay to put up with it'. You may want to change the order of the words to suit yourself or you may want to use variations on this idea. It is best not to repeat yourself exactly on several different occasions; if you do so you risk starting to sound 'false'. It may be easier for you to use 'I get', or 'I become' instead of 'I feel', for instance, and some people find it easier to use the words in a different order — you could change it to 'When you . . . I get . . . because . . .'. For example, 'When you leave your clothes in the lounge I get angry, because I spend a lot of time cleaning it up.' It doesn't matter about the order of the words as long as all the necessary information is given.

This method is very different to saying, 'You make me mad when . . .'. No-one can *make* you angry, or sad, or frustrated. Rather, you *become* angry, sad or frustrated because, amongst other things, the behaviour which you feel that way about goes against your own value system. You don't *have* to act that way and *you can control your emotions if you really want to*. It is simply not true to say that someone *makes* you angry.

You *choose* how you respond to the behaviour of other people. This is most evident when you respond in different ways to the same behaviour from two different people. If you are like most adults, you put up with far more annoying behaviour from other adults than you are prepared to put up with from a child. Yet it is possible to treat them both the same way.

If a child refuses to alter a behaviour that affects you in some way, you may have to add some information about what you intend to do about it. More is said about this in chapter 8 on consequences but, in general, you should make sure that you can carry through on what you say.

Sometimes a child will do something that angers you, or annoys you, or even disgusts you, but you are unable to explain how that behaviour affects you in a concrete way. When this happens, you can be sure that a value is involved. Sometimes value differences affect you only when they are carried too far. For example, it may normally not bother you if your child's bedroom is untidy but when you can smell it as you pass by you may become very annoyed indeed.

When you want to speak to a child about a problem concerning a value difference, state *once* what your value is and, maybe, explain why you hold that value, then allow the child to work it out for himself. The important thing about values is to make sure that your actions match your words.

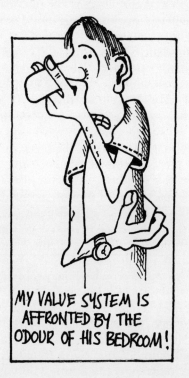

MY VALUE SYSTEM IS AFFRONTED BY THE ODOUR OF HIS BEDROOM!

Separate the child from the behaviour

One of the problems with criticising a child is the tendency to judge her according to her behaviour, and to then insult her in attempting to correct it. In other words, we often have trouble separating the person from the behaviour. For example, saying, 'You must be stupid to do a thing like that' is very likely to cause trouble, not because of the behaviour, but because of the direct insult to the child. All that was heard was 'You must be stupid', and this may do lasting damage to his self-esteem. 'That was a stupid thing for you to do' is a much better way of putting it, because at least it criticises the behaviour rather than the child. It could even be taken as praise because it implies that the child is above that sort of behaviour. While there is no doubt that it is the child who is acting in an unacceptable way, he himself is not unacceptable. It follows that if the child is ok but his behaviour is not, then it is the behaviour that you should criticise, and not the child.

The danger in identifying a child with a single behaviour is that you may hang a negative 'label' on her and in doing so actually cause the behaviour to continue — 'My father thinks I am stupid so I may as well act that way'. Separating the child from the behaviour is therefore very important, and you can do this by stating your disapproval of the behaviour without inferring that the child 'is' the behaviour. The easiest and quickest way to get this across is to use the 'I feel ... when ... because ...' method, or to simply say, 'I love you and accept you, even though I do not accept that behaviour' or, 'You're ok but that sort of behaviour is the pits'.

When value differences are involved you may be able to come to some arrangement whereby the child does not do whatever it is when you are around, or does not do it in the house. This is a bit difficult when the problem is something like a particular hairstyle, but it can work with many problems.

If a teenager is playing a tape that you object to very loudly, you may say to him, 'That tape is offensive to me because of the language. I believe that you are entitled to listen to it if you want to, but I don't believe you have the right to force me to listen to something I find offensive'. This kind of statement is usually very effective, unless the child is deliberately trying to annoy you. If that is the case then all you have done is tell him how annoyed you are.

Stick to one problem

Criticising others often leads to arguments because one criticism is brought up, then another, then another. It is sufficient for a child to accept one criticism at any one time. She may be willing to accept criticism of a particular behaviour, but will

undoubtedly become defensive if the criticism becomes an attack from too many directions at once, or if another behaviour comes under fire as soon as the first one is dealt with. Alway remember: one time — one topic — one criticism.

Be positive and give encouragement

One often hears parents say things like, 'I praised him for doing the job but he still got upset and stormed off'. This is probably the result of using the word 'but'. The so called praise was probably something like, 'You did that job very well *but* the corners are still dirty'. This is a negative criticism even though it separates the person from the behaviour and gives all the necessary information. The word 'but' seems to dispose of all the words before it to leave only those words which follow it. In this example, all the child would hear is,

'The corners are still dirty'. A much better way of putting it would be, 'You did that job very well *and* it would be even better if you cleaned right into the corners'. This praises the work, suggests improvements and encourages the worker.

Therefore, one way of practising positive criticism is to substitute the word 'but' with the word 'and'. Another way is to say how well the job has been done with the equipment the child used and ask if there is anything else he needs that could help him improve the job. You could also say how well the job was done this time compared to his earlier efforts and perhaps comment on how more experience will further improve it.

Summary

Being assertive means giving the same respect to the rights and needs of others that you expect to get from them. It also means letting others know when their actions cause you a problem while remembering that it is your problem and that you need to take this into account when approaching them.

Before criticising the behaviour of a teenager, think about just how it affects you and why it affects you because so many of the things we argue about are value differences that have no real effect on us. Each person values the things that help her meet her needs but adolescents can be quite confused in what to value, and so experiment to find their own set of values. Most will gain their values through the example of their parents and sometimes they will see different values to what their parents intended them to see.

When it is necessary to criticise a teenager's behaviour, remember the four Rules of Feedback:

1 Give all the information necessary about the problem without demanding any correction;
2 Separate the child from the behaviour;
3 Stick to one problem;
4 Be positive and give encouragement.

CHAPTER 5

COMMUNICATING WITH TEENAGERS

The rules of talking

When we are very young we learn how to talk, and we grow up believing that, because we can talk, we can communicate. But there is a huge difference between being able to talk and being able to communicate. Two people may talk to each other for quite some time yet, if they are not talking the same language, there may be no communication.

In this chapter, I will discuss the link between talking and communication by going over some of the 'rules of talking' that help us communicate effectively. Relationships should improve with improved communication because it is through communication that we help each other to solve problems. It is also through communication that our children's problems can become known to us, and if we know about them we can help solve them. Many many ideas could be included here, but I trust the following will be enough for our needs.

Eye contact

Most people become uncomfortable when they feel that they are being stared at, or when someone tries to 'outstare' them during a conversation. This applies equally to children, especially adolescents, and indeed is one of their pet hates. I have often heard teenagers talk about how teachers and social workers do it 'Just to make us feel rotten'. They also say things like, 'They think if I look away, I must be lying'.

Many parents also use eye contact too much and this may be because they too were brought up to think that 'Sincere people can look you straight in the eye'. This, of course, is absolute rubbish; the opposite is probably closer to the truth. Many people learn to 'stare and lie' simply because they know that they will be condemned if they look away; many people are able to stare 'eyeball to eyeball' while telling lies.

Judgements can be made from eye contact, but these should only be about things which aid communication, like whether or not the young person is listening and whether or not he seems to understand what is being said. It is important not to stare at him for too long, however, simply because it is inconsiderate to cause discomfort in this way. While eye contact is necessary it is certainly not necessary to hold it throughout an entire conversation. To be stared at without relief can be very unnerving. If someone feels uncomfortable talking to you then you can hardly expect that person to want to share her problems with you.

Some people try to talk without making any eye contact and this generally hinders communication. Eye contact should be encouraged, but used correctly. It should not deteriorate into a staring competition; its purpose is to aid communication.

I find that if I become angry I am inclined to fix my gaze on the other person, and the more angry I become, the more I stare. So staring can be quite aggressive, and a young person who feels threatened by this type of staring may well try to avoid eye contact altogether, or avoid the person who does it altogether.

If your child always attempts to avoid eye contact, talk so he can see that you are not staring all the time:

1 Make sure that you look away and back, even if you only glance down at your hands for a second or so, or at the ceiling, or at anything except directly into his eyes.
2 Show by example that it is possible to have comfortable eye contact and to give relief from 'the stare'.
3 Become aware of just how much you stare when talking to all people and what effect this seems to have on them and the conversation.

The main point here is that eye contact should not be used to win a contest that is just another part of a power struggle, it should be used to help people communicate, by passing on meaning.

Communication is a 50–50 deal

Most of us spend a lot of time talking to people and trying to impress them with our stories, jokes and experiences. Young people are the same and are probably even more interested in talking than adults. They spend a great deal of their time just talking among themselves, about all sorts of things. Unfortunately, many people simply 'talk' without taking much notice of whether their audience is interested or not. Most young people learn to get out of the habit of 'talking for talking's sake' because their peers insult and 'rubbish' them for it. A great number, however, continue the habit into adulthood and become 'party bores'.

The best way to ensure that young people are interested in what you are saying is to talk about their interests. Usually you can pick up clues about what interests them, and if you have trouble doing this there is always the immediate situation to talk about. If you are travelling in a train with strangers, for example, you might comment about the train, the view, how long the trip takes, or how comfortable the seats are. You could even talk about how hard it is to start a conversation on long trips. Even the seemingly silly question, 'What do you know?' can be a very good conversation opener.

The clues to a young person's interests are sometimes very obvious from the clothes they wear, the music they listen to and who they are with. There are also many subjects of interest to all teenagers that can be used to start a conversation, such as school, work, music, clothes, home, brothers and sisters, nosy parents and so on. It might be necessary to learn something about the things they are interested in, so you can contribute to a conversation in a meaningful way. This may be as simple as watching a particular television show, or taking a look at a music magazine.

ASSUME A TRANCE-LIKE STANCE TO INDICATE THE CONVERSATION IS BORING

All people use non-verbals and noises to hint that they are not interested in the conversation, although it is rare for anyone to come straight out and say the story is boring. The non-verbals will become stronger and stronger to try to get the message across if needs be. People are likely to fidget, to look out the window, avoid eye contact, constantly look at the time, make noises of agreement in a bored tone of voice, make sounds of impatience at how long it is taking, or stare down at the floor with a 'trance-like' expression. Even if a topic is of interest to both parties, conversations should average out as 50–50 deals. If one person consistently 'hogs' the time she may well earn the title of bore. The rule is talk *and* listen, about 50–50.

Not all conversations will be 50–50, because one person may need to talk something out or use the other as a 'sounding board'. Even so, the average amount of talking and listening over a number of conversations with the same person should be 50–50. Listening is just as important as talking when it comes to communicating with others, including children, and in some conversations it is extremely important. The most pleasant people to talk to are often those who are good listeners:

1   If you don't listen to other people, you cannot understand what they are really saying;
2   If you cannot understand what they are really saying, you do not grasp their meaning;
3   Communication means 'an exchange of meaning', so if you do not grasp their meaning, there is no communication.

Some people go into too much detail when they speak. This quickly turns others off, and they soon learn not to ask anything at all because the long-winded, blow-by-blow description they will have to listen to if they do will waste their time and bore them to tears. Even though others may be interested in what is being spoken about, they probably do not want to hear every little detail.

If you suspect you are someone who talks too much, try giving a short answer next time you are asked a question and take note of what happens. People will generally ask another question or indicate in some way that they want to hear more. This is far better than turning them off with too much detail. However, don't be put off by kids claiming that you are preaching or 'going on and on'. Many children make this claim if more than two words are put together on a topic that they don't want to hear about. If you have something to say, say it and remember that they can still hear even with their fingers in their ears.

Talk on the same level

People of all ages can ruin a perfectly good comment by adding an insulting word at the end of it. The rest of the sentence may make a lot of sense, and might have been taken notice of if it wasn't for that very last word. Many arguments and fights start because of the way some people add insults to what they are saying. If an insult is included in a comment, it will probably be the only thing the other hears. It is not surprising that comments like, 'What do you think, stupid?' usually result in arguments. This is not of course because an opinion was sought, but because someone has just been insulted. The reply will probably be defensive, and may well also contain an insult as revenge. Words like 'Stupid', 'Slut', 'Idiot', 'Birdbrain', 'Fatso' and many more can and do cause unnecessary arguments and resentment. To avoid this simply avoid using insults at the end of sentences. Sometimes one person will deliberately insult another in order to upset him, or it may be that by now the insult has been used so long it has become a habit. Either way such behaviour will damage relationships.

Suggesting that people talk on the same level is usually taken to mean 'use words that the other person can understand', which of course is necessary for communication. But talking on the same level also applies to the physical positions of the people involved. If the other person is sitting — you sit. If the other person is standing — you stand. If you stand to talk to someone who is sitting, you dominate the situation which may make the other person feel very uncomfortable. If the other person stands to dominate you, and you want to even things up again, just stand up. On the other hand, it may be necessary to sit on the floor to make the arrangements comfortable for both.

Even a piece of furniture can be used to make a conversation uneven. Sitting behind a desk may be used to indicate one's 'higher position', but any piece of furniture can be used to put distance between people. So if you want a close and friendly conversation with someone, don't sit behind a desk or place furniture between you.

As mentioned, talking on the same level also means making sure you use words that the other person understands. There is no point at all in using words that are not understood, you may as well talk in a different language. Adults often complain about adolescents using words that they don't understand, but adolescents don't understand a lot of the words adults use either. All this is bound to cause arguments that could easily have been avoided by using more simple words.

Some people also like to 'show off' their knowledge in front of others, which is another cause of unevenness, but far fewer arguments would occur if people did not state their personal opinions as facts. Very few real facts are known, because most things we are aware of are matters of how we see them from our own experience. Two people can look at the same scene yet argue about what they see. Even if they agree on what they see they can argue about what it means. We may also repeat something as a fact when it was just something that we were told, or we read in the newspaper, or we saw on television. If we find out later that it isn't true then we have to admit to being wrong, although many of us try to bluster or bluff our way out of doing so.

None of us likes to admit we are wrong and the simple solution is to stop repeating hearsay and opinion as fact. There are ways of doing this which can be easily practised. It is simply a matter of how we word what we repeat, and especially how we begin a sentence:

- 'I think that ...'
- 'I believe that ...'
- 'I was told that ...'
- 'The last time I saw ...'
- 'I read in the paper this morning that ...'
- 'On the news last night ...'
- 'They say that ...'

These openers give the impression that you are passing on information which may or may not be true, so if the information does turn out to be wrong, it is the information which is wrong, not you.

Questions

Most people become annoyed when they are asked a lot of questions and this applies especially to adolescents. Sometimes just one question can be annoying, particularly if it is difficult to answer. You are probably aware, for example, how the question, 'Why are you in a bad mood?' can actually put you in a bad mood if someone persists in asking it. But a statement like 'You seem to be unhappy' would not usually annoy you because it implies concern, and because it does not call for an explanation you are more likely to give one.

All questions can be changed into statements by changing a few words around and these statements are more likely to get answers from someone who doesn't like questions. As in the above example, this is because statements do not demand answers, rather, they leave it up to the individual to decide whether or not to respond.

Asking a child to explain her misbehaviour may meet with a very negative response, if only because it is quite hard to give an explanation which doesn't lead to more questions. Approaching the subject with something like, 'I don't understand why you did that', will usually be more fruitful.

The question, 'How did you get from there to here?' demands an answer and may even lead to a power struggle. But, 'It puzzles me how you got from there to here' doesn't demand an answer and cannot easily be used to begin a power struggle. It is also more likely to produce an explanation. While statements do not demand answers they can put a lot of pressure on a child to change all sorts of behaviour, even the way he communicates.

Sometimes it is necessary to ask questions, however, and sometimes you will want more than a 'yes' or 'no' answer. In the latter case you need to ask questions that cannot be answered with a 'yes' or a 'no'. To do this start with a word which asks for information, that is, how, where, when, why, what or who. Practise asking these sorts of questions. You may still get a one-word answer, like the famous, 'Dunno', but you increase your chances of getting a longer answer by using information-gathering words.

Starting and ending conversations

People nearly always start and end conversations using non-verbal messages. The list of non-verbals is seemingly endless, so only a few will be discussed here. Non-verbals used to start a conversation include eye contact, smiling, moving closer, bumping into each other etc. When it comes to talking, people at first tend to stick to safe topics, like the weather; if the response is favourable they may risk another comment. Another common opener is the familiar:

'G'day, how are ya?'

'I'm goin' well, how are you?'

'Great, just great.'

These two characters are not really concerned about each other's health, they are simply finding out whether or not they can talk, and this is a safe and accepted way of doing it.

Whereas most people are able to start a conversation, some have great difficulty in knowing how to finish one. We may endure many long uninteresting conversations that use up our time because we don't know how to 'get away' politely. Some people also have trouble noticing when another person wants to finish the conversion, and just keep talking on and on. The most common signs that a conversation is about to end are:

- Looking at the time;
- Standing up from a seated conversation;
- Taking a step towards the door;
- Closing a book that has been a reference during a conversation;
- Putting a hand on the door knob;
- Allowing a long pause in the conversation.

People use many different non-verbal signals to say that a conversation is finished and it can be very annoying if someone ignores, or fails to recognise, these. Indeed, some people will not take the hint at all and have to be told straight out that the conversation is over.

Offensive talk

A chapter about talking would not be complete without some discussion of offensive talk. Some of the words here may offend you, however it would be rather difficult to discuss this topic without giving some examples.

People often refer to 'clean' words and 'dirty' words, even though those words may have the same meaning. For instance, it's alright to say intercourse but not fuck. So we might ask the following questions: 'How does a word become dirty?' and 'How do you clean a dirty word?'. If something is dirty, you can clean the dirt off. Because it is not possible to clean a word, it is not possible to dirty a word. These meanings exist only in our minds; the word itself is only a sound that we put meaning to. It seems, however, that some 'dirty' words are miraculously made 'clean' by simply using them in a different way. For example, if a young man approached a woman in the street and asked for a 'screw', he may get a slap across the face, because that would be 'dirty', but if the same woman worked in a hardware store and the same young man approached her for a 'screw', she would simply reply, 'What sort?' The word 'screw' has no meaning in itself, it is simply a sound that people put meaning to. Its meaning exists in the mind of the person who said the word and in the mind of the person who heard it. In normal conversation we hope that both people have the same meaning for the same word because it is only when people understand each other's meaning that communication occurs.

People who don't understand each other may have to talk about it until they can work out what each means. They may still not agree but at least they both know what is meant. Many a comedy has been staged around the fact that the meanings of words exist only in the mind, yet we still tend to see words themselves as having meaning.

I cite the following story about an incident from my childhood to illustrate that words only have meaning in the mind, and that understanding occurs when two people have the same meaning for a sound.

When I was about eight years old, I wanted to buy a little orange-coloured ice-cream, sold at the corner store. I didn't know what to ask for, so I asked my older brother what the name of the ice-cream was. He said, 'They're called Penny Farts'. When I asked the shop assistant for a Penny Fart, she naturally didn't know what I was talking about. However, instead of getting offended, she talked to me to find out what I meant and, after my explanation, gave me the ice-cream. After that, whenever I went to the corner store and asked for a Penny Fart, the assistant would hand me a little orange-coloured ice-cream, because 'Penny Fart' now had the same meaning for both of us. (I have since realised how embarrassing this may have been for her when there were other customers in the shop!)

The words people find offensive seem to have different meanings to different people. Sometimes people will have difficulty saying why they find a word offensive, or 'dirty'. As well, a particular word may offend people when it is heard in the street, but not when it is used in an hotel. It all depends on where the word is spoken and who hears it.

The police must have trouble at times trying to decide whether to charge someone with offensive language, especially when the same words can be heard on television or in stage plays. Meaning may change over time, so that words can become 'dirty' or 'clean', or even lose their meaning altogether. For instance, the words 'piss' and 'fart' are old English words that were quite acceptable at one time. These words have changed from being 'clean' to 'dirty'. To be called a 'bugger' was a great insult years ago, yet now it seems to have little or no meaning. This is a word that has just about lost its original meaning.

I read somewhere that the word 'fuck' originated as follows:

Many, many years ago, when a man appeared in the old English law courts on a charge of carnal knowledge, the court officer announced that 'This man appears For Underage Carnal Knowledge'. Gradually, however, this was short-ened to, 'This man appears on a charge of F.U.C.K.'.

If this is true then it is easy to see where the association between sexual intercourse and the word 'fuck' came from.

This discussion would not be complete without mention of the word 'slut'. This word is offensive to most women, and yet they can be quick to use it against each other. Some men use the word as the ultimate insult to women because there is no equivalent that can be thrown back at them. Equality of the sexes would be moved a long way forward if the word 'slut' changed meaning to apply to any person, and not just to a woman.

Many children use offensive words for shock value, and they achieve that aim when you get upset by it. The use of offensive language is another type of misbehaviour, so the four purposes of misbehaviour mentioned earlier apply here as well. If the purpose of all misbehaviour is to stir up a particular reaction in you, and you are aware of this, then you can choose to react differently.

Summary

Just because we talk does not mean we communicate. Many factors affect whether or not we communicate and how well we communicate. Some of these things are as simple as eye contact, which may be wrongly used to judge a person's sincerity. Eye contact should only be used to aid communication.

Talking relationships work best if they occur on equal footing. This means both parties should speak for about half the amount of time and on the same 'physical level'. It is also important not to ask too many questions, or at least to ask appropriate questions. It also helps if you can recognise the non-verbal signs people use to start or end a conversation.

Offensive words should be regarded in the same way as any other misbehaviour because their use can have the same four purposes. However, offensive words are only offensive because of the meaning that you place on them.

CHAPTER 6

THE ADULT EMERGING FROM THE CHILD

The parent, adult, child theory

Most people have at least some idea about the different theories on human behaviour, and some people believe they are all rubbish. I don't know about the theories being all rubbish, but I do find some of them handy when I want to gain some understanding of the things people do. For instance, earlier on I used some ideas about the causes and purposes behind misbehaviour, to give some meaning to it and therefore to understand it better. According to the method I used, misbehaviour can be understood using the following headings:

1   Attention
2   Power
3   Revenge
4   Inadequacy

As well as providing some understanding of misbehaviour, the method can be used to help you gain control of your situation by urging you to decide how you will react to the behaviour of others. But now I want to use a different theory altogether, one that I have found particularly helpful in trying to understand what is happening as the teenager is becoming an adult. Most of the people I have spoken to on this subject have found it very interesting and useful in understanding both their children and themselves.

In some ways it seems a bit strange that we, as parents, find it so hard to understand what is happening to, and within, a child who is going through adolescence, because we have all been through it ourselves. We appear to have forgotten what it was like, or perhaps we believe that because we got through it alright, so will our children. Fortunately, the majority of kids do come through adolescence relatively unscathed, but, unfortunately, when it is their turn to bring up kids they will probably be just like us and will have forgotten what life as a teenager is like.

You may now be faced with a kid who is asking all sorts of questions about things she previously took for granted, who is doubting your word on many of the things she used to accept without question. Even her new friends are given more credibility than you are. She regards rules as 'stupid' and continually questions them. She may even claim that all rules should be done away with, and that people should be able to do whatever they wish — 'Who made the stupid rules anyway, and why do I have to follow them, I didn't have any say in them.'

Questions about rules, and especially questions about the reasons behind particular rules, are not easy to answer, perhaps because you don't really know why they were made yourself; they've just always been the rules. This is hardly going to satisfy an adolescent, however, who may leave you with no better answer than, 'Because it is, that's why', or 'Because I said so'. Although this questioning of your rules and values may be annoying, it is healthy. Besides, it will probably only be annoying if you don't know the answers. People don't seem to mind answering questions when they know the answers, but it can be a different story when they do not.

Before we go on with the new theory, I want to digress for a moment to talk about a mini-theory on rules and why they are made. You may find it helpful when kids are asking awkward questions about why rules are made if you try to relate all rules to two main themes. These themes are that rules are made for safety reasons, or that they are made to give people a fair go. They may also be a mixture of the two. I am quite sure that every sensible rule will fit under one or both the headings. The themes of safety and a fair go include emotional and psychological safety and justice as well as physical wellbeing, and you will find that even little rules will come under one of these criteria.

The three parts of every person's make-up

Now back to the adolescent, and why it is healthy to question things that we believe. I have based the following explanation on the ideas of Dr Eric Berne, author of the book *Transactional Analysis*. First of all, it is helpful to think of every person's psychological make-up as having three major parts:

1   Feelings
2   Thinking
3   Rules of behaviour

These three parts exist in all people of all ages. Dr Berne gives each one of those parts a name:

1   CHILD
2   ADULT
3   PARENT

These parts do not refer to an actual child, an actual adult or an actual parent, but to the three parts of any person of any age. The words CHILD, ADULT and PARENT are given the following meanings.

CHILD

The CHILD part refers to feelings and emotions, and includes all wants and desires. The CHILD part is loving, wanting, playful, spiteful, creative, intuitive, hurting, sorrowful, manipulative, jealous, joyful and all other things to do with feelings. It is the laughing and the crying, the tantrum and the playful, as well as the selfishness and the frustration.

CHILD

ADULT

The ADULT part is like a computer; it simply gathers information by using words like why, where, how, what and when. It uses the answers to these questions to make decisions about what to do. The decisions made by the ADULT computer are decisions made without feeling because feelings do not belong to the ADULT part, they belong to the CHILD part. However, in a well-balanced person, both the CHILD and the PARENT have a big influence on the decisions made by the ADULT.

ADULT is the part that makes decisions about what to do. It is also the part that should look at the results of decisions made to decide whether or not the action was appropriate. ADULT gathers information from the CHILD (what you feel like doing), from the PARENT (what you should do), and from the environment (what is happening and what others think), and then makes a decision. By itself, ADULT has no conscience and no feeling; it is a computer-type decision-maker.

ADULT

PARENT

PARENT

The PARENT is the knowledge of what is right and wrong, of how things should and should not be done. The PARENT is like a tape-recorder which has recorded everything we have ever learnt about how people should be treated and how life should be lived. Most of what is recorded on our PARENT tape came from watching our own parents when we were very young, and listening to what they said. Some of what is on our PARENT tape is learned from other people, such as school teachers and relatives. So what is recorded on our parent tape makes up our rules and value system. The bulk of it was recorded when we still believed that our parents were always right because they knew everything, so that everything they did must have been right as well.

The difference between PARENT/Parent, ADULT/Adult, CHILD/Child

You will have noticed that the words parent, adult, and child are written in two different ways. This is to separate the actual parent, as a parent, from the meaning that Dr Berne gives to the PARENT part of every person. This will also apply to the child and CHILD as well as to the adult and ADULT. Whenever I refer to a child I mean an actual child, but whenever I refer to the CHILD I am referring to that particular part of every person; it could mean the CHILD part of an eighty year old.

The actual parent has feelings and can think, but the PARENT part of the parent can be thought of as the tape-recording of the rules he uses as a guide to live by. The adolescent can be in a PARENT mood whenever she is talking about rules, or making noises about how people should act. The adolescent has a very strong parent tape in her head, but has reached the stage where she questions the quality of some of what is recorded.

The actual adult person has feelings and acts according to rules and principles, but the ADULT part of the adult (or any person) is the actual information-gathering and decision-making part. The adolescent is in the ADULT mood whenever he is seeking information in order to make a decision. He may seek this information from his parents, or from other relatives, friends, teachers, books etc. If this child's parents want to be a major source of information then they should make sure they can answer his questions, or he will seek information elsewhere. His parents may not like talking about things like AIDS, sexually-transmitted diseases (STDs), abortion, drugs, homosexuality, vaginas and penises, oral and anal sex, or the meaning of some words, but it is better that they take the trouble to learn about these things so that they are able to discuss them with their child, rather than have him pick up what he can from the walls of public toilets. When he wants to learn about these things it is the time for his parents to give him information on which he can base his decisions. The decision-making itself is the function of his ADULT part, and it is this part which is undergoing great change. The ADULT part must grow and mature if the adolescent is to have control over his life and make responsible decisions. We will go into how you, as parents, can play a part in this in subsequent chapters.

Every child has a PARENT part and an ADULT part because every child knows right from wrong, and can make decisions. Every child also has a CHILD part that is no different from the CHILD part of her parents. The actual child has feelings and emotions, just like adults, and it is the feelings, the wants and needs of the adolescent that make up the CHILD, just as they do in all other people.

The term 'childish' may require some explanation to avoid confusion, because as well as child and CHILD, we have childish. If a person is acting in a CHILD mood when it is not appropriate, that person is being childish. The same person could do the same thing when it is appropriate, and those actions would not be childish. For example, an adolescent throwing a basketball around in the lounge room is being childish, but if he does this on a basketball court there is no problem. To throw a ball around in the lounge is a

CHILD and childish act, to throw a ball around on the basketball court is still a CHILD act, but it is not childish. Throwing the ball around the court is an appropriate way of having fun, and having fun is a very natural and healthy part of CHILD.

Dr Berne uses drawings to help explain his ideas. He uses three circles arranged vertically, with PARENT at the top, ADULT in the middle, and CHILD at the bottom. However, this arrangement could be taken to be the order of importance, although he did not mean it that way. In an attempt to impress that each part is of equal importance, I have arranged them horizontally. This first drawing represents a well-balanced person of any age:

The well-balanced person has a good proportion of guidance, decision-making, and feelings. Such a person has physical and emotional needs and wants (CHILD) which she seeks to satisfy. In her head she carries rules and values as to how she should and should not act (PARENT) in attempting to satisfy the needs and wants of the CHILD. Therefore, decisions are constantly being made because the CHILD wants satisfaction while the PARENT tape sets restrictions. This is where the ADULT part comes in and gathers information from both 'sides' so that a decision can be made which allows the PARENT part and the CHILD part of the person to live in peace. To be able to make these decisions, the ADULT part needs to be strong, and it only becomes strong through practising decision-making. The more decisions a person makes, the more likely he is to have a balance between the three parts.

Consider the following drawings:

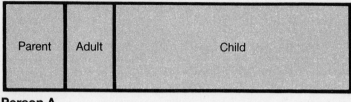

Person A

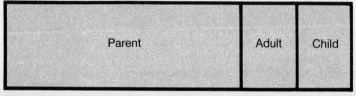

Person B

No-one stays in the same mood all the time, especially adolescents, but because I want to keep things simple for this explanation, I will ignore such complications and take the drawings to represent a person. An adolescent in the mood of Person 'A' may be making plenty of decisions but these are dominated by the CHILD. In other words, she is mainly following her urges, feelings, emotions and wants in deciding what she is going to do; there is very little notice being taken of the information coming from the PARENT, which would limit the wants of the CHILD.

If we wanted to draw a person who is really being 'childish' we would draw his mood in the way Person 'A' is drawn. The reason why we say that Person 'A' is acting childishly is because he is following his own feelings without allowing for the needs of others. He very likely would throw a tantrum if what he wanted was refused, or perhaps he would use abusive language and generally 'play up'. But there is also a positive side to this drawing. We might have forgotten that the CHILD part also encompasses feelings of love and affection. It also means the creative genius. We can see that when an adolescent is in the CHILD mood she may be at her most lovable.

Person 'B' is the opposite. This person is very much obsessed with rules and doing everything right. His feelings are suppressed and he has very little fun. He generally does not express his emotions and so he does not show much love. He may do a lot of good things for others, but this is due to parental influence rather than from thinking things out for himself. As well, Person 'B' always knows the right way to do everything. He is clearly dominated by what is recorded on his PARENT tape. He makes few genuine decisions because what is in the CHILD has very little influence, and what is on the PARENT tape is never questioned. Although he is seen as being a 'good' boy because he is so obedient, he is not what we would call a well-balanced person; he lacks ADULT and CHILD.

The role of the ADULT part of a teenager

Look at this drawing:

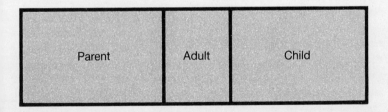

Here we can see more easily what happens as a young person changes into an adult. We see that the ADULT is beginning to emerge but needs to be exercised in order to grow. As I have said, the only way to do this is to make decisions. To do this intelligently the ADULT must gather information by asking questions and observing others. The process goes round and round in circles, the more decisions the ADULT makes, the stronger it gets and the more decisions it wants to make. The more decisions it wants to make, the more information it needs to gather. The more successful the outcomes of decisions, the more confident the person becomes about making decisions.

FLEX THOSE
ADULT MUSCLES

Questioning the PARENT tape

We still need to explain why it is healthy for an adolescent to question everything that has been recorded on her PARENT tape if most of the information there came from watching, and listening to, her parents. Remember, everything you saw your parents do and everything you heard your parents say is recorded on your PARENT tape as the 'right' way to do and say things. However, much of what a child sees and hears may be performed by parents who are in a CHILD mood. How is any child able to distinguish between what is coming from the PARENT of his parents and what is coming from the CHILD of his parents? When you were recording on your PARENT tape, were your parents behaving seriously (as 'parents'), or were they in a fun mood and just 'fooling around'? Either way you were recording their actions as part of your guidelines for living. So, what is going on to the PARENT tape as it comes from the parents might have been passed on for generations, even though it may have originated from someone's CHILD. Some quite silly traditions are created by generations of people passing 'the right way to do things' from PARENT to PARENT. Not only silly traditions but also destructive beliefs, like those that continue to split the Jews and the Arabs, or those behind the conflict in Ireland. The hope for the future in these things is that people will come to question what is being passed down, that young people will start to question some traditions, and want change. It may be useful to stop and think about how much of what you believed as a child you have since found to be rubbish? How much of what you were taught as being truth have you since learnt is wrong? You could start with Santa Claus and the Easter Bunny, or the many changes that have occured in religious beliefs and observances since the early 1960s.

Summary

Questioning rules is a natural part of being a teenager and parents need to be able to explain why the rules exist. To do so it is helpful to refer to the headings 'safety' and 'a fair go'.

According to Dr Berne's ideas, there are three parts to the psychological make-up of each person and these he named PARENT, ADULT and CHILD. The three parts roughly equate to the rules of behaviour, the gathering of information, and the feelings of a person, and at adolescence the ADULT part is emerging from the child and needs to be exercised if it is to grow strong enough to balance the other two parts. This is achieved by making decisions after gathering information from the CHILD, from the PARENT, and from the environment. It is both necessary and healthy for a young person to question everything that is on the PARENT tape in her head.

CHAPTER 7

HELPING TEENAGERS MAKE ADULT DECISIONS

Responsible behaviour

In the previous chapter I put forward the idea that there are three parts to the psychological make-up of each person, and that one of these parts is the decision-maker, called the ADULT, which needs plenty of exercise if it is to grow strong enough to function effectively. In this chapter I want to suggest some ways you might help your child develop a strong ADULT.

Every day of your child's life, from the minute he was born, you have been helping him to become a responsible, independent person. The amount of help you gave in the early years was intense because he was learning to do so many things. He was learning to walk, to talk, to feed himself, to run without falling, to ride a bike, to tie his shoelaces, to comb his own hair, as well as countless other things. Each thing he learned to do for himself put him that much closer to becoming fully independent; here was one more thing he didn't have to depend on other people to do for him. Hopefully, he also learnt to do these things in a responsible way, and by this I mean that he can now be trusted to go about his activities without interfering with others.

You probably found that the first five years, during which you helped and guided your child, was followed by a long period when most of her learning seemed to occur at school. During this long stretch on the road towards independence, you may have dropped into a pattern in the way you treated your child, a pattern that came from years of knowing what seemed to work best in her case. Now, suddenly, after a few years when nothing much happened because most of her training occurred at school, peace seems to vanish into thin air as you once again become her main source of guidance. Your child is an adolescent, and this requires you to treat him in an entirely different way; the pattern that has worked for you up until now is no longer relevant. If you are confused by the shifts in your child's behaviour and attitudes, and your authority seems to have gone out the window, you are no different to many other parents. Maybe you were expecting this, but were caught unprepared by the suddenness and/or the extent of the change.

Adolescence is the next stage in your child's growth towards independence and responsibility. It is a time of intense training as she begins to think seriously about her choices in life and to make decisions that will affect her future. Adolescence is, in other words, the time for exercising the emerging ADULT part of the personality.

The adolescent stage can loom large if this is your first experience of it. But you should keep in mind that there is not much advantage in having had previous experience because each child is quite different and has quite different problems. Many parents comment that their first child got through adolescence ok, and though they treated the next one the same, things did not go so smoothly. For this reason you need to remain open-minded and flexible in your approach to each child.

Unlike beginning school, there is no set age for the start of adolescence. Changes in your child's behaviour may lead to many fights and troubles, and sorting these out can keep you so busy that you haven't time to think about why all this is happening. This is when you need to force yourself to stop and take notice of the purpose behind the behaviour, which, as you may recall, will fall into one of the following four categories:

1 Power
2 Attention
3 Revenge
4 Inadequacy

This is the time to change the way you are reacting to your child's behaviour. It is the time to ask, 'Whose problem is it?', the time to stop and take charge of your situation as a parent. One of the problems arising from fights and other troubles you are having with your child is that you may come to think of him as being 'irresponsible' and incapable of making sensible decisions. You should guard against this because just the opposite is likely to be true. Your child has simply reached a stage where he wants to make his own decisions; he may feel that he is not being 'allowed' to exercise his emerging ADULT.

If the purpose behind your child's behaviour fits into one of the aforementioned categories, then the time has come for her to take greater control of her life. The conflict between you can be positive if it is used to point to areas where exercising her ADULT can occur. This is far better than attempting to 'win' fights, because if you succeed your child is likely to become submissive, inadequate, and resentful. You could say that your problems are the result of your child making too many decisions, and this is why there is so much trouble. You may even think that he should be stopped from making his own decisions because he makes so many bad ones. And of course it is true that just because a teenager is making decisions doesn't mean that the ADULT is being developed — decisions can be made without much thought at all. Many decisions made at adolescence do not look very far into the future, and don't seem to make much sense. Such decisions are probably taken to satisfy wants and feelings and so arise from the CHILD rather than from the ADULT. This is also true when the decision-maker has no intention of accepting the consequences of her actions.

Many actions are not the result of decisions made now at all, rather, they result from decisions made in the past. What appear to be decisions may simply be automatic reactions, reactions which occur without thinking. Like riding a bike, or swimming, many things we do become 'automatic' because we do them so often. If you drive a car, for instance, most of your driving is done without thinking, and you may even be one of those people who find they can work out their problems better while they drive. This would be impossible if you had to think about every action to do with your driving.

Young adults are very self-centred and their automatic reactions are based around this fact. They naturally act to satisfy their own needs and wants, without giving much thought to how their actions may effect others. You may as well accept this as normal, because it is. Most teenagers grow out of it as they become more aware of the consequences of their actions, especially what other people think of them. Hopefully, they will continue to grow towards making decisions that genuinely consider others' needs as well as their own.

The three parts of responsible behaviour

Before we go on, I will take some time for another explanation. It is pertinent at this point to briefly set out the relationship between decision-making, behaviour, consequences and responsible behaviour. Again, I am oversimplifying this somewhat but it is still useful as preparation for discussion with superlogical adolescents. You never know, perhaps one of his questions will be, 'What is responsible behaviour?'. What follows should help you out in situations like that.

There are three parts to responsible behaviour. These are thinking, doing and consequences. We are presently concerned with decision-making, which comes under the thinking part of responsible behaviour because it should be the result of thinking about particular circumstances.

The simplest way to put the relationship between decision-making, behaviour, consequences and responsible behaviour is this: 'I have acted responsibly if I decide to choose a particular way of solving a problem, I do what I decided to do, and I take the consequences of my actions'. I use this explanation with adolescents because it gives them room to turn seemingly irresponsible behaviour into responsible behaviour, and so encourages them to keep trying. Adolescents usually act according to the immediate situation, and may choose whatever is available in that situation to satisfy their immediate needs, although this may badly affect other people. This is why adults tend to say that adolescents are irresponsible but, according to the above explanation, the behaviour is not irresponsible until the adolescent avoids the consequences. Thus she has the opportunity to save the day, by accepting responsibility for her actions.

I will leave this short explanation with the following thought. The act of stealing, in itself, may not be irresponsible but avoiding the consequences of such action may make this way of solving a problem irresponsible. According to the above explanation, if a person steals, he still has the opportunity to act responsibly by admitting to the theft and taking the consequences.

The thinking part

The following rules make up what we term 'responsible behaviour' and the phrases in capital letters point to areas where the ADULT can be exercised:

- SOME THOUGHT MUST BE GIVEN TO DIFFERENT WAYS OF SOLVING A PROBLEM. The different ways of solving a problem are referred to as 'the alternatives';
- A DECISION MUST BE MADE BETWEEN THE ALTERNATIVES AFTER SOME THOUGHT HAS BEEN GIVEN TO THE CONSEQUENCES OF TAKING EACH ONE;
- The chosen alternative should be carried through;
- The consequences of that decision should be accepted;
- SOME THOUGHT SHOULD BE GIVEN AS TO HOW IT ALL TURNED OUT.

Note that the decision taken does not have to be the 'best' or the 'right' alternative — it is far better to make a 'mistake' than to avoid making a decision at all. The most important thing is that a choice between alternatives is made, which means that the ADULT is exercised. Exercising the ADULT comes from thinking about alternatives, thinking about the consequences of each, and making a choice. It also entails reflecting on how the whole thing turned out.

The difficult part about teaching this process to a child is to allow her to make mistakes, or make choices that are different to those you would make. Naturally you want to protect your child from making mistakes, and perhaps you are inclined to think that your way of doing things is the best way — it works for you so it should work for your child. In the past he has encouraged you to think like this because he also believed that your way was the best way. When it comes to exercising his ADULT, however, he must be allowed to think up his own alternatives and make his own choices.

Before going on to make some suggestions on how to give adolescents room to exercise their ADULT, I must point out that you will have to exercise your own ADULT first, because the suggestions which follow are alternative ways for you to start encouraging your child to do so. You know what you can and cannot do, so you will have to consider the different alternatives and decide which one you think is the most appropriate for your situation. You should be prepared to follow through with your decision and to take the consequences of your actions. In other words, it is important that you act responsibly. You should remember that thinking about how your decision is working out is part of acting responsibly and that you may have to make new decisions as circumstances change.

You should also bear in mind that just as you are the expert on your problems, your child is the expert on hers. Because you live your problems, you are the one best placed to work out some ways of dealing with them. And the same applies to your child. She knows better than anyone what she can cope with, and so she should be consulted when you are trying to decide within what limits she should be making decisions for herself.

What are 'limits'?

If your child is to make decisions within set limits, we must decide exactly what the word 'limits' means. Limits are quite difficult to describe because they are very much tied to values, and everyone has a different set of values. The difference between values and limits can be seen in the way we are prepared to tolerate the different *values* of other people to a certain point. That point is the *limit* to which we are prepared to tolerate those other values. Limits are therefore as numerous as values; when we talk about limits, the number of things we must consider is endless.

Just because the list is endless doesn't mean we can't talk about setting limits, it simply means that we have to use more general terms. Examples to give you some ideas on how to set your own limits are included here. Knowing your own limits is vitally important when you are trying to set them for an adolescent.

People can be a little inconsistent when it comes to limits. While they condemn adolescents for pushing the limits most adults do the same thing in more 'acceptable' ways. Trade unions are constantly pushing to broaden the restrictions on their members; drivers consider the speed limit to be the normal speed, or go a little above it; taxpayers are always looking for loopholes in the tax laws; and the 'sickie' may only be taken when you are well enough to enjoy it. The point is that no matter how narrow or how wide you set the limits, your teenage son will push right up against the edges. He will occasionally break a 'rule' to test if it really is the limit, or whether it is just the first line of defence. Therefore, the limits decided on must be the limits and must incur some kind of consequences if they are exceeded. Consequences are the subject of the next chapter so we will not go into them now.

Below are some examples of how you can set limits. You will see that limits involve making rules and deciding what is meant by certain words.

Example one: It may be decided that your teenage daughter can go out four nights a week to any structured activity. This allows her to decide whether or not she will go out and on which four nights of the week she will do so. She can also decide where she is going as long as she observes the rule that it must be to a structured activity. Your only concern is that she keep within the set limits.

Example two: It may be decided that a structured activity means that there is something definite on and that there is adult supervision. This allows your son to decide between a wide range of activities, but at the same time may call for discussion as to whether a particular activity falls within the limits. Again, you only have to keep an eye on the limits in relation to the activity. For instance, does late night shopping come within the limits? In this case you may decide that there is something on — shopping — and that there is adult supervision because shopkeepers and the general public are present. But what happens when the shops close?

Example three: It might be decided that your daughter can find her own way to and from activities but that it is too dangerous to walk after dark. This means she can make her own decisions about times and transport and allows for discussion about co-operation in regard to the latter.

Example four: It may be decided that your son is to take his lunch to school each day, and that you will supply him with sandwiches. He likes cheese so you will give him cheese sandwiches each day. If he wants a change from cheese, it is his responsibility to put what he wants in his sandwiches on the bench before you make his lunch. This meets the requirement about lunch, and allows your son to make decisions about what type of lunch he gets.

These four examples demonstrate that limits don't have to be the very extreme of what you can stand. They can be commonsense rules that are geared towards encouraging the exercise of the ADULT, while taking into account the needs of the whole household.

Discipline

It is appropriate that the word 'discipline' get a brief mention here, even though it is often thought that discipline should be talked about in relation to consequences, because discipline is frequently associated with punishment.

Discipline means to keep within certain limits. Rewards and punishments are commonly used to keep people within limits and this is what is meant by 'being disciplined *by* someone'. What we are interested in, however, is encouraging young adults to be *self-disciplined*, that is, to keep *themselves* within set limits. The space between the limits is the area available for a teenager to exercise her ADULT. In other words, you should be allowing your child to make all decisions for herself within whatever limits are set down. The tricky bit is deciding what the limits should be.

Setting the limits for your family

Your knowledge of your teenage son in particular and of the way your family works in general plays a large part in deciding what limits are appropriate for your son. By 'appropriate' I mean that the limits should match his age and capabilities.

In general, an adolescent is capable of deciding more than her parents allow, but is not capable of deciding as much as she thinks she can. However, keeping in mind the three parts which make up responsible behaviour, it may be that the limits should allow for a particular problem to be worked on. For example, if your son is not able to think up more than one way of solving a problem, he may not be ready to be exercising his ADULT in the sense that is meant here. You may still decide to encourage him to make choices but decide also that you will provide direction as to what he should or should not be doing.

Problems areas

Some adolescents/people find it difficult to choose between several alternatives. Others may be fine when there are only two choices available, but are hopeless if there are any more than this. Whatever the case, some people literally agonise over decisions they should make, or go to great lengths to avoid making them in the first place. If you are aware that this is a problem for your child then you will have to make allowances when it comes to setting limits. Maybe you will need to arrange for only two alternatives to be available until she feels comfortable even making a choice. You could then arrange for three possible alternatives until she feels comfortable with this, and so on.

Other adolescents/people are able to think up all sorts of possible solutions to a problem, and make very sensible decisions, but then do not follow them through. They do not act on their decisions, and they may not stick to agreements even when they had the main say in what was decided. This problem can have many causes. Perhaps, for instance, the agreements were not fairly made because your son felt he had to agree, or maybe he couldn't tell you what he really thought because he believed you would become angry if he did. It might be that he is afraid of failing, in which case he will need a lot of encouragement, or perhaps he doesn't really believe you are sincere in letting him run his own life. Whatever the cause for his hesitancy when it comes to acting on his decisions, you will need to take this into account when deciding the limits of his decision-making. It could also be that you need to examine your own behaviour and attitudes carefully.

Probably the most common problem when it comes to decision-making is an unwillingness to accept the consequences of one's actions; this amounts to irresponsible behaviour. Your daughter may deny she did something, admit that she did it but refuse to accept that it was her choice, claim that if it hadn't been for the presence of others she wouldn't have acted the way she did, and so on. If this kind of thing is happening, you will have to make provision for it. You can do this by ensuring that your daughter has no choice but to accept responsibility for her actions, either by relying on natural consequences, or by making sure that you have control over what was decided, and are prepared to carry this through.

Suggestions for setting appropriate limits

The following suggestions are made assuming that your son hasn't already taken the law into his own hands and is ignoring your position as a parent. If you have an adolescent who is 'doing as he pleases' then the next two chapters, 'Consequences' and 'Letting Go of your Teenager', may be more appropriate to your problem.

The first suggestion when it comes to setting limits is to take it slowly, that is, you should not suddenly tell your child that she can now make all decisions which affect her for herself. Doing this could be disastrous, especially if she hasn't had much practice at decision-making, and especially if she tends to blame others for her actions. You may need to take it slowly at first by allowing her to make small decisions, while giving her plenty of encouragement to keep trying. Getting thrown into a deep swimming pool is not a good way to learn to swim, and entering a marathon is not a good way to start exercising one's muscles.

You may feel quite comfortable about handing over some of the decision-making to your son, or you may feel that you need to gain some confidence in his ability to handle decision-making before you hand much of it over. In the latter case you could allow him to make decisions in certain things to set your mind at rest before allowing him to make more responsible decisions. This does not mean that he has to agree with you; what it means is that you need to satisfy yourself that he can make decisions and 'face up'. You might decide that he can make decisions about things he is genuinely willing to take responsibility for. To do this, of course, you need to discuss with him what areas he thinks he can handle, and you have to be prepared to let him take the consequences, whatever they turn out to be. Working on this suggestion gives him the opportunity to reach high, make mistakes, and receive encouragement to keep trying. You could also decide to allow him to make his own decisions on value differences first: how tidy he keeps his room; who his friends are; his school achievements; and anything else that does not affect others very much, if at all. Or you might decide to let him make decisions about things that affect others in the family, such as:

- What jobs he will do around the house;
- When he will play his cassette recorder;
- Where he does his homework;
- Whether he has a pet;
- What his bedtimes will be.

You may decide that he can make all decisions that affect him but, until you gain confidence in his ability to think through the consequences of his actions, he will have to discuss his decisions with you before putting them into action.

Helping teenagers make decisions

Once you have set the limits within which your teenage daughter can make decisions for herself, you need to decide how to go about helping her to make decisions, at least to start with. Once you have gained some confidence in her decision-making ability, it may well be that only sometimes will she consult you about her problems. I suggest that whenever a problem which involves her comes up, you ask her what she sees as being the alternative ways of solving it. Remember, it is important not to make any comment about any of the suggestions until it comes to actually choosing between them. When your daughter has run out of ideas, but

not before, you might suggest another way, if you can think of one. However, any suggestion you make must be put as just another suggestion, no better and no worse than the others, and *not* as the way you think is best. If you present your suggestion as the best one, she might choose your suggestion because she thinks she has to, or reject it simply because you suggested it.

You could then ask her what she thinks would be the likely outcome of the different suggestions and encourage her to make a choice. She may try to avoid making a decision by asking you to choose, but if this happens it is best to just continue to talk about the possible consequences of the alternatives and be firm that the choice must be hers. It may be necessary to reassure her that it is fine to make mistakes, that it is part of making decisions.

One problem with allowing your son to make decisions is that you have to allow him to take the alternative he decides on, even though you may see it as a very poor choice. You might think that another alternative is the obvious choice, but try to avoid saying so, because you must be genuine in allowing him to make his own decisions and his own mistakes.

When a teenager makes a choice between alternatives that are all 'right' alternatives, she cannot really take credit for doing the right thing. After all, to make a good choice, at least one of the alternatives has to be wrong. For example, if she needs money to buy a cassette recorder and the alternatives she thinks up are:

- Saving up her pocket money;
- Doing extra jobs in order to earn extra money;
- Getting a part-time job;
- Borrowing the money.

These are all right alternatives that do not really involve a choice between right and wrong. A real choice to do the right thing would require that one of the alternatives be, for instance, to steal the money.

Sometimes a teenager will suggest a wrong alternative just to see what your reaction is. This is a way of testing whether you are genuine about considering all alternatives, because stealing *is* an alternative. Whether or not it is an alternative you approve of, or choose, is not the point. It is possible to get the money by stealing and, therefore, it is an alternative. If you jump up and down about it and rule it out as an alternative, you are doing at least three things:

1 You are showing that you are not genuine in considering all the alternatives open to your son;
2 You are removing the opportunity for him to choose between right and wrong;
3 You are increasing the likelihood of him stealing the money, if only to prove to you that it is an alternative.

If an alternative that you consider to be 'way out' is suggested, you should simply acknowledge that it is an alternative by saying something like, 'Yes, that's another way', and then deal with it when the two of you are considering the consequences of each suggestion. If your daughter teases you by implying that she will choose the alternative you don't approve of, you can say that the choice is hers, and that you have no objections as long as she is willing to take the consequences. Usually, if your reaction is not what she expected, she will drop the alternative as, 'just a joke'.

If no possibly contentious alternatives are mentioned, it may be that your son is afraid to suggest them. But there is nothing to say that you can't make such suggestions. If your son expects only 'right' suggestions from you, why not throw in a 'wrong' one sometimes? Of course there is always a chance that he will choose that suggestion, leaving you to wonder whether to stand aside and respect his choice. The chances of him doing this, however, (especially if it is one of your suggestions) are very small.

Summary

Parent's begin teaching their children to be responsible independent people from birth, but at adolescence the emphasis of parenting is very much on helping young adults make their own decisions and to do so in a responsible way. 'Responsible behaviour' is seen as consisting of three parts and the ADULT part, which is used to strengthen decision-making ability, is the thinking part. This means to think about the alternative solutions to a problem, to choose an alternative and to monitor what is happening as the choice is acted on.

A young person should be encouraged to make decisions within the set limits and these limits should be made having regard to her demonstrated responsible behaviour. As a parent you should accept the alternative chosen and allow the consequences to happen, even if it is not the alternative you would have chosen.

CHAPTER 8

CONSEQUENCES

Rewards and punishments

Most parents would agree that their main aim is to bring up their children to be responsible and independent people, even though they may not agree on how to achieve this. Disagreement on how to get young people to act responsibly can be a real problem when it comes to consequences. Two very caring and concerned parents, who share ideals about parenting, may disagree bitterly on what are the appropriate ways to deal with misbehaviour.

Most people learn how to be parents through the example of their parents, who learnt from their parents, and so on. Parenting is one of those skills that people are just somehow supposed to be able to pick up from their parents, and pass on to the next generation. Because of this 'hand-me-down' way of learning how to bring up kids, a great variety of methods exist, falling somewhere between two extremes. On the one hand there is, 'The kids will do exactly what I tell them, or else' attitude, and on the other the, 'I just let them do their own thing' approach. Both of these extremes can produce the same effect, however, that is very irresponsible and unhappy young people.

Fortunately, most parents operate well away from these extremes. This does not mean, though, that they don't have problems knowing what to do when their children misbehave. And this brings us to the subject of consequences. To a great number of people, the word 'consequences' means 'punishment'. Saying things like, 'You will have to take the consequences' generally means that there is some kind of punishment looming. I have found that most children believe the word consequences means punishment and that they interpret the word 'behaviour' as meaning something wrong or bad. This is probably because they are used to hearing these words used in relation to being naughty.

For our purposes, the word behaviour means any action we do, good or bad, and a consequence means something that naturally or logically follows on from our behaviour. What follows on may or may not be pleasant, that is, it may be a good consequence or a bad consequence.

Everything we say and everything we do has some effect on something else. In other words, every behaviour has a consequence of some kind, and that consequence will influence whether or not we continue to do whatever it was that caused it. A good consequence is likely to encourage us to behave in a certain way again, but a bad consequence is likely to result in us dropping that behaviour. It is what happens as a result of our behaviour that teaches us how to behave; we keep doing what pays off and we drop what does not. For example:

- It doesn't pay to put my hand into flame because it hurts, therefore I am not to do it again.
- If I leave a mess around, people get upset, so, if I don't want to upset them, I clean up my mess.
- If I am pleasant to people, they're pleased to have me around. So, if I want to be accepted, I should try to be pleasant.

For a long time parents were urged to use rewards and punishments to keep control of their children, to get them to

BEWARE THE "REVENGE CHILD"

behave 'properly'. The idea was that good habits are formed when good behaviour is rewarded and bad behaviour is punished. This is still a very common way of bringing up children, and does have its place, but there are certainly dangers in using this method to maintain control.

If you rely on rewards and punishments to 'shape' the behaviour of your children, you need to be very careful to ensure that proper rewards are given for ordinary, everyday 'good behaviour', otherwise children are likely to feel discouraged and 'inadequate'. The other side of the coin is that if the punishments outnumber the rewards, children can become vengeful. As well, because you are the one who controls the rewards and punishments, you are the one with all the power, which could produce a power struggle or a revenge situation. You need to keep an accurate record of the balance between rewards and punishments to avoid the pitfalls involved in using this method of training your children.

A further problem is that you need to be sure that a child sees the reward as a reward and not as a punishment. It could be that the reward was not as big as he expected and so he feels disappointed (punished). In contrast, a punishment can become a reward if the punishment is not as big as he expected. We can see that the balance between what will work and what will not is very delicate, as well as unclear.

Things can also become very complicated when you consider the attention-seeking child. Punishments require you to give attention to negative behaviour and rewards require you to give attention to positive behaviour. At first glance, this may not seem like much of a problem, but what about when an attention-seeking child is quite satisfied with the attention, whatever way it goes? In this case, you could easily find yourself in an extremely stressful situation.

To try to control a child by using rewards or punishments is to rely on her wanting rewards, and being afraid of punishments. This means that if she is not willingly doing what you want, she is doing it because she doesn't want to cop the punishment. It might also be that if she can avoid the punishment she will misbehave again. Even if you threaten a punishment she is afraid of, the method will only work if the punishment can be applied. If your child can outrun you or she avoids getting caught in some way, or you are not even aware that she has misbehaved, it is useless even threatening her. In other words, if the child does not fear the punishment, or there is little chance of getting caught, or she does not intend to accept the punishment, you cannot be sure that she will obey your rules.

So, to be effective, whatever is threatened has to be feared by the child. If the threat made isn't feared, he can say, 'Go ahead, make my day' or, 'So what?' or, 'Make me!' and laugh at your increasing frustration. He knows that you have no authority unless he gives that authority. Such a situation can be very stressful indeed if you persist in trying to force obedience.

Your child may believe that the only thing she does wrong is to get caught, because it is only when she gets caught that she gets punished. This could be another reason why she tends to blame you for her misbehaviour. After all, there is some logic in her thinking that if you hadn't caught her she wouldn't have been punished. The punishment may then be seen as being punishment for getting caught, and be teaching her to become better at avoiding being found out. She has probably 'got away with it' many times before anyway, so the odds are pretty good, as long as she is careful about not getting caught.

Consequences

There are two kinds of consequences: natural consequences and social consequences. Natural consequences are those which naturally follow on from a behaviour. Social consequences are those which occur because someone steps in to make them happen. Social consequences are usually referred to as logical consequences, but I prefer the term 'social' because it implies learning things like co-operation, and getting along with other people.

Natural consequences are known to everyone. They include things like:

- If your child doesn't eat, he will get hungry;
- If your child goes out in the rain without a raincoat, she will get wet;
- If your child puts his hand in a flame, he will get burnt;
- If your child eats too much before going on a swing, she will get sick.

Natural consequences happen without outside interference. They occur as a natural result of certain behaviour and a child soon learns this. An adolescent child knows about natural consequences, he doesn't need to be reminded that he must eat to avoid getting hungry.

Some examples of social consequences are:

- If your child is late for school, she will be reprimanded by the teacher;
- If your child doesn't study, he will not pass his exams;
- If your child misses too many days at work, she will be fired;
- If your child picks fights, he will get a fat lip;
- If your child doesn't go to hockey practice, she will not get a game.

Social consequences are not like natural consequences because they may or may not happen. A social consequence occurs if another person steps in to make it happen. In the above examples, the teacher would have to reprimand the student for being late, the boss would have to dismiss the worker, the other fighter would have to throw a punch to produce the fat lip, and so on. It is important to keep in mind that social consequences do not always happen because, for example, the teacher may get distracted or may feel very tolerant on that day, the boss may decide to give your child another chance, or the big right cross might just miss its mark.

For social consequences to be effective in teaching people how to behave, it must be obvious that they are logically connected to particular behaviour, as in the above examples:

- It is logical that a child will get into trouble for being late to school;
- It is logical that poor exam marks result from not studying enough;
- It is logical that the boss will get sick of paying someone who doesn't come to work;
- It is logical that a 'lucky punch' will get through sometime.

To sum up:

- Natural consequences do happen.
- Social consequences may or may not happen, depending on whether another person steps in.
- For social consequences to be effective in teaching people how to behave, they must be logically connected to the behaviour.

Some differences between rewards and punishments and consequences

I t might appear as though good and bad consequences are just another way of saying rewards and punishments. To a certain extent this is true, good consequences are rewarding and bad consequences are punishing. Nevertheless, rewards and punishments are also quite different to good and bad consequences and understanding these differences is very important if you want to have control of your situation as a parent.

Quite often, the difference between rewards and punishments on the one hand and consequences on the other is in the way something is said:

Example one: 'If you do your homework early you can go to the disco.' In this example, going to the disco is the reward for doing the homework early because it implies that the parent is giving permission to go to the disco as a reward for doing the homework.

Example two: 'Doing your homework early should leave you time to go to the disco.' In this example, having time to go to the disco is a consequence of doing the homework early and implies, 'if that is what you want'.

The first and most important difference then, is that consequences encourage a child to be responsible for his own behaviour, and to have self-control, whereas handing out rewards and punishments make it the parents' responsibility to control his behaviour. Rewards and punishments can allow the child to blame you for the outcome of the behaviour but consequences can be shown to be the result of the way he behaved.

Some kids go to the extreme in putting the responsibility on their parents and can only be trusted to behave when they are being watched. Some will come right out and say that it is the job of other people to control their behaviour, therefore, if no-one is around, it is open slather. I have known adolescents to claim that the victims of their crimes were at fault for not being more careful, or the police were at fault for not being there to stop them, or their parents were at fault for not 'making them behave'.

A second major difference between rewards and punishments compared to consequences is that rewards and punishments are decided by someone and need not have any logical connection to the behaviour. Consequences, on the other hand, can be more easily placed under the child's control, and do have to logically connect to the behaviour. Consider the following examples:

Example one (punishment): 'If you don't do your homework, you will not get any dinner.' There is no logical connection between dinner and homework, neither is there a natural connection. The threat of missing out on dinner is being used in an attempt to 'outweigh' the homework in order to give a choice between the two.

Example two (consequences): 'If you do your homework early, you will be able to take your time over dinner.' This leaves the choice with the child and there is a logical connection between time and the way things are arranged.

A third difference between rewards and punishments and consequences is that the former lead a child to believe that she has no control of her life. In contrast, consequences let her know that she does have control of her life, simply because consequences change as her behaviour changes.

A fourth difference is that rewards and punishments must come immediately after the behaviour if they are to be effective, which means that the behaviour must be detected each time. If rewards and punishments are to be really effective, a full-time guard would need to be employed. On the other hand, consequences may take some time to occur, but this does not matter. Moreover, every behaviour has a consequence regardless of whether or not it is detected by other people.

Changing to the use of consequences

The main obstacle for most people when it comes to changing from using rewards and punishments to using consequences is sorting out who should be controlling who. Many of the problems between parents and adolescents arise from parents believing they are responsible for controlling the behaviour of their almost-adult children. This belief leads to two types of power struggles:

1   Struggles which result from parents believing they are to blame if their teenage children misbehave;
2   Struggles which result from parents believing they know what is best, and that they have a natural authority which their adolescent children should obey.

Although such parents believe that they have the responsibility and/or the right to control their children, their children are usually well-aware that neither of these things is true; they know that no-one can 'make' them do anything. However, by constantly blaming their parents, children can manage to keep them believing that they *are* responsible for controlling their behaviour. Some children will keep their parents busy jumping from one crisis to another, from one confrontation to another, trying to 'make' them behave properly.

Because all power struggles involve both authority and power, it is time to pause and explain what I mean by these words. In the past, it was generally believed that authority was something which came from above, and that it was to be obeyed without question. But the fact that people can decide whether or not to obey a rule or law shows us where authority really comes from — it comes from below. Most people obey laws, but it is the very fact that they can *choose* to disobey them that shows us where authority really comes from. Guns, tanks and the threat of death cannot make people obey if they decide that they no longer give authority to the law. Children are no different, in any given situation they either give authority or they do not; no-one can make them do anything, and they know it.

Some points about what power is and how it is used to maintain control of people are:

- Power is having control over something that someone needs or wants;
- What is needed or wanted can be anything at all, from basic safety to luxuries;
- To use power to control someone means to supply what the other needs or wants in return for obedience. In other words, rewards and punishments are employed to control the other's behaviour;
- Continued obedience depends on the other's continued need or want;
- Who holds the power usually depends on who is the biggest and strongest;
- A person who is controlled by power usually resents the person who has the power.

It is very unfortunate that many parents trying to control their children still rely on the fact that, if nothing else works, they are the biggest and can hand out a light slap, a hefty smack, or a heavy beating. Even those parents who claim that they have never smacked their children may be getting obedience through threatening to use their larger size. While they may not actually carry out this threat, their children are certainly aware of it and their parents, at times, are quite happy that their size is to their advantage. But there comes a time when parents are either no longer the biggest, or when just being the biggest no longer works. By this time, their children have quite likely lost all respect for them.

Relying on physical power to keep control can be a habit that is hard to break, particularly if you don't realise you are doing it. A simple example here is when a mother tells her small child, 'If you don't go to bed I will tell your father when he gets home'. This mother is threatening the child with the greatest power on Earth, apparently, 'father'. Another example is when a parent stands in the doorway of the bedroom until the child cleans up his room. The child cannot leave the room without being big enough to push past the parent. A further problem with using power is that it keeps the child's attention on how it can be beaten or avoided and away from the behaviour itself. In other words, 'How I can do what I want to do and get away with it?'.

The use of rewards and punishments is just another form of power control, because whoever hands out the rewards and punishments controls 'who gets what'. Children may learn to behave in a certain way in order to gain a reward or to avoid a punishment, but they will probably also resent the person who decides these things. Children may be glad to get rewards, but may hate having to crawl to get them. A small child may think it's good to get a lolly for going around to the shop, but she only has to stop wanting a lolly and the bribe becomes useless — 'Didn't want your old lolly anyway'. The same thing happens when teenagers decide they don't want to go to summer camp if it is constantly used to get them to obey rules.

The practical use of consequences

If an adolescent is to become a responsible person, he must be allowed to experience the consequences of his actions. He must not be allowed to avoid the consequences, neither should he be saved from them. It can be very difficult to stand back and allow something unpleasant to happen to your child, who you are supposed to protect, but to constantly save him from the unpleasant consequences of his behaviour will not help him protect himself in the long run. Of course this does not mean that you should allow him to have unsafe sex or crash a car. It would be totally irresponsible to stand back and allow real harm to come to one's child, if it could be prevented. More will be said about this in the final chapter, but for now I am talking about things which are not life-threatening.

Nearly all adolescents know how to behave well, that is,

they know what is acceptable behaviour and what is unacceptable behaviour. They may need to learn new ways of handling some situations but they do know 'right' from 'wrong'. Given the right incentive, all adolescents are capable of self-control. Even the most troublesome teenagers can be very loving and responsible when they want something, which shows that they are capable of responsible behaviour when it suits them.

As a general rule, the consequences of misbehaviour should be known to an adolescent before she decides on some course of action, so that the consequences can be a matter-of-fact happening, needing little or no discussion. In this way the behaviour itself, a negative, need receive little or no attention. You can thus be relieved of the burden of being seen as the penalty-imposer, and the consequences rest where they belong, with your child.

Consequences are more effective if a young person has some say in what they should be. You may find that there is far less conflict if the rules of the house are decided between you and the kids. This seems to be because the rules can then be discussed; they are not seen as belonging to you only. 'The rules' become external to everyone and are owned by everyone.

If you really want to go deeply into using consequences, try getting your teenage son to set his own, then do some bargaining. You will probably find that your son will set down much harder consequences than you would, you can then suggest that they are too harsh. Long consequences, for example, are an invitation for trouble, because a week is a long, long time to an adolescent. A social consequence that lasts longer than a week is asking to be broken, especially if it cuts him off from his friends.

An important aspect of getting an adolescent to set the consequences is the discussion process, where she is encouraged to examine her behaviour and its effects on other people and things. Sometimes this discussion will reveal that sufficient natural conseqences followed the behaviour, so there is no need for social consequences as well.

Generally speaking, it is a good idea to leave some time between the behaviour and the discussion, because you may be too upset to calmly talk about it. Moreover, adolescents may be more ready to fight than to talk soon after doing something wrong, or may not be capable of talking things out. Say your 15-year old daughter comes home very late and very drunk, but still able to hang on to a bottle of booze. The look on her face says her only thought is, 'Oooh, I'm crook'. Obviously, there wouldn't be much point in trying to discuss consequences at this stage. Her most likely response would be to throw up on the carpet. There will be time enough to talk in the morning, for now just steer her into the bathroom, so she can throw up in an area that is easy to clean. Then, if she doesn't need medical treatment, put her to bed. The morning will bring its own consequences, so the time to talk is after the natural consequences are over.

One of the most crucial points about getting kids to set their own consequences is that they are more likely to stick to them if they have agreed that they are appropriate. What form consequences take is not the important thing, what is important is that they are set and followed through. This makes teenagers feel better about themselves and puts them in control of their lives. Of course, they don't always stick to the consequences, but this can be dealt with as a separate issue. The point here is that those kids were probably defying consequences before anyway, so anything that might improve the situation is worth a try.

Putting the responsibility on the adolescent to decide his own consequences encourages him to take a look at his behaviour and to take responsibility for it. Most adolescents will jump at the chance, but some will try all sorts of tricks to get you to set the consequences so they can duck out of taking responsibility. Your child may do this to test whether you are genuine about allowing him to take responsibility for himself. This often takes the form of not being able to think of a consequence and asking you what it should be. Unless you are very careful, he will succeed in getting you to set it down, which would defeat the whole purpose of attempting to get him to do so. It can take a lot of practice and patience to get some kids to accept responsibility for their behaviour and to realise that it is causing problems. Unfortunately, kids are rescued from most natural consequences of their behaviour by their parents. This 'rescuing' will be the subject of the final chapter.

Discussing a teenager's behaviour with her, in order to work out consequences, sometimes reveals many natural and social consequences which occur without you having to do anything, or will soon reveal consequences which can be applied. For example, your teenage daughter stays all night at a friend's house, without arranging it with you first, and you decide to ask her to set her own consequences. The first thing to do is to get her to decide what part of her behaviour caused problems to other people, and how those people were affected. She can then be told of any effects she had not mentioned, like the cost of the phone calls made to try and trace her, or the time spent by the police in taking a missing person's report, the time of hospital staff checking attendance sheets, and your own loss of sleep. As noted, the best consequences are those which come up when discussing them. Usually, they can involve trying to repair any damage done or paying for any expenses involved, like phone calls and/or petrol costs. In this example, who is going to let the police know your daughter has returned? Perhaps she should do this as part of putting things right. Or perhaps she could do something for you so you can catch up on some sleep.

There are times when consequences can be used to bring you and your teenager closer by learning things together. Perhaps the discussion led to drugs, and showed up how little either of you knew about, say heroin. In discussion you might decide that you both have to collect information about the drug so that you can discuss it in a couple of days time. This way of doing things helps a teenager realise how his behaviour is affecting other people, and affecting what other people think of him. As I said earlier, acceptance and approval are extremely important to teenagers. They can discover first-hand how their behaviour is affecting others if they are encouraged to focus on this, rather than have their attention swung on to defending themselves against a parent who is out to punish them.

Very troublesome teenagers can make discussing their behaviour and its effects almost impossible, especially when they may lie so much that you have trouble believing anything they say. If this is the case it is best to stick to what you know happened and take into account only those things that can be verified. When some kids tell you something, the only thing you know for sure is that they can still talk. They may not accept *any* suggestion that their behaviour has affected others, and may succeed in diverting your attention onto the behaviour of other people. Sometimes you may have to abandon talking and swing into action by using the co-operation trade-off.

The co-operation trade-off

It is not uncommon for a child to tell an adult, 'You can't make me do anything', and this is indeed true. But it is also true that the adult can say the same thing to the child. In most cases, however, an adult is reluctant to carry through with the trade-off that this implies.

The popular way of expressing the trade-off idea is, 'You scratch my back and I'll scratch yours'. The problem here is that this implies the child must do something before getting what she needs or wants. I believe the ideal would be, 'Let's scratch each other's back', because this implies co-operation. This may mean that you end up doing most of the scratching and getting little in return, but if this happens you can revert back to 'You scratch my back and I'll scratch yours'.

There is an important difference between the ideal mentioned and the clear bribe. Like so many things, the difference lies in the way it is said. This can be shown in a couple of simple examples. A clear bribe would be, 'If you clean up the mess you made in the lounge, I will give you the money to go to the disco'. This is an attempt to offer something as a reward for doing what you want. A trade-off in the same situation would be, 'You said before that you

A TRADE-OFF

want money for the disco tonight and I mentioned that I want the mess in the lounge cleaned up. Perhaps we can make a deal'.

Using trade-offs can be a powerful way of teaching kids the value of co-operation, because losing it can fit under any of the consequence titles. For instance, an argument could be made that losing the co-operation of people is a natural consequence of not co-operating with them. It could also be argued that anyone who is unco-operative must expect to lose the co-operation of others. These are social consequences because the very word 'co-operation' infers at least two people helping each other in satisfying both of their needs. Children learn to co-operate by experiencing the benefits of co-operation, and the pitfalls of not co-operating.

Some points worth noting about the co-operation trade-off are:

1   Make sure that you have complete control over what you are trading with;
2   Never threaten something you are not able to follow through with;
3   Never threaten something you are not willing to follow through with;
4   Sit down, have a cuppa, and make a list of the things that you do for your child, beginning with calling her in the morning and going through the whole day — washing, ironing, cooking, cleaning, driving, pocket money, finding things, making excuses, writing notes for her, and so on.

Normally it is only necessary to use small trade-offs, but if the going gets tough you may have to use any or all of your co-operation. When you use the co-operation trade-off, it is crucial that you do it in a calm and friendly way, with no hint of insult or putdown, because you want to keep the attention on co-operation, not revenge.

Remember that the greatest advantage you have at your disposal is your attention and approval. Parental approval/disapproval is so powerful that it should be used very carefully indeed. It affects the self-esteem of the young person and therefore his life and happiness. To receive a disapproving look from a parent can be far more hurtful to a child than a smack. A cross word or tone of voice can be a far more effective consequence than any other punishment because it implies disapproval. Most of the time it isn't necessary to say anything if your child is aware that you disapprove, the feeling of being disapproved of is powerful enough. Remember when the two year old got to the stage where a smack had no effect, but the same child could be devastated by a cross word. Even when kids grow up they don't change much in this regard. Most adults feel terrible when someone disapproves of them. It is also worth keeping in mind that most adults feel lousy if a superior growls at them, but if the growl becomes a roar, then they are likely to want to fight back. Adolescents are the same, show them disapproval and they are likely to think about their behaviour, roar at them and they are likely to rebel.

To impose a punishment or introduce a hefty consequence can divert attention from this natural approval/disapproval process and be less effective because the focus is now on your right to impose punishment. The attention is taken away from the child's behaviour and is focused on the parent–child relationship.

Approval is something that all people, not just children, need rather than want. Sometimes they may not want it at all and may greatly resent needing it. This is what should give you encouragement to continue in your job, even when your adolescent children are rejecting attention and approval. Just be there for them when they do want some help, and take the opportunity to strengthen your relationship. It is when your child is hurt that you can become the healer, just as you were when, as a tot, he skinned his knee while playing and returned to you to kiss it better.

Sometimes teenagers play pretty rough with their misbehaviour and this may mean leaving home after many arguments, and much bad feeling. Some almost seem to want to get kicked out by making things intolerable. They may go a bit wild once they taste full freedom and do things that you strongly disapprove of. You should never show approval of things you disapprove of; kids are usually well-aware of their parents' values and can be quite disappointed if they act contrary to them. Once again I would point out that there is no need for a lecture, you can remind your child of your values, in very definite terms if need be, but you must let him know that it is his behaviour you disapprove of, not him. If he has left home and misbehaves when visiting, you could give him a gentle reminder like, 'As you know, John, I don't approve of that sort of behaviour and I would prefer that you don't do it here'. A stronger stand could be, 'You are well-aware that I don't like that sort of behaviour around this house, or in my presence. If you want to do that sort of thing do it somewhere else, not here. You are welcome here anytime but I don't want that sort of behaviour imposed on me'. An even stronger stand could be, 'How you and your friends act away from this house is your concern, and you will have to take whatever consequences arise from it. Other people and the police can deal with that, my concern is for our relationship and how things work in this house. I do not want any of that behaviour in or around this house, and I do not want any of the people you do it with to come here. Just leave us out of it'.

Your child will stumble many times out there in that big world while trying out different values and becoming independent, and will suffer hurts as a consequence. Most of these she will want to fix herself and will become quite angry and resentful if you try to help. The idea is to wait until she approaches you, because then you are helping her to solve her problem. Remember that if you approach her, you are the one with the problem. I suggest that a good way of controlling your parenting in such a situation is to leave the door open for when your child shows that she wants, as well as needs, your attention and approval, by asking your opinion.

Summary

People learn what to do and what not to do according to the consequences of their actions. If good things happen, they will act the same way again, but if bad things happen they will probably not repeat the behaviour. This process works best if the result of the behaviour is a direct consequence of it and is not an introduced reward or punishment. Using rewards and punishments places the power over your child's life in your hands, rather than his. In contrast, if natural or social consequences follow a teenager's behaviour, she can see more easily that a change in her behaviour will bring about a change in consequences. She will also know that she does have some control over her life.

Natural consequences do follow certain behaviour and are usually well known to teenagers. Social consequences may or may not come about because they require someone to step in to make them happen. Therefore, you can use social consequences as unavoidable consequences in correcting unacceptable behaviour and to impress on your teenage son the necessity for co-operation if the household is to run smoothly. Sometimes a co-operation trade-off will be necessary to maintain that smooth household.

Even social consequences can be placed under a teenager's control if she is allowed to set them herself. Again, she will learn that she can have as much control over her own life as anyone else does. This is only effective if she is allowed to experience the consequences of her actions.

CHAPTER 9

LETTING GO OF YOUR TEENAGER

Drawing it all together

In the previous chapters we have discussed problem-solving, limits, responsible behaviour, consequences and some general communication topics. The time has come to draw all this together as we consider the difficult subject of 'letting go'. It is not too much to say that letting go is the whole reason for the turmoil of the teenage years. The breaking-away process that begins at puberty and ends with the young adult leaving home will inevitably be accompanied by turmoil and even pain.

It is a difficult time for you, as parents, partly because the family is changing and partly because it is so hard to know how much and how fast to let go, at what rate to expand the range of responsibilities you hand over to the budding adult. I hope this chapter will clear up some of the problems in this area. We will also look briefly at the concept of the adolescent's search for identity during the breaking-away period.

Helping a teenager to build an identity

Some parents are a little puzzled when they hear that their adolescent child is searching for an 'identity', or is going through an 'identity crisis'. This process can be very painful and can last for years. You might say something like, 'But my kid knows who she is, she's my kid, that's who she is'. Well, perhaps her pain comes from knowing that she has always been 'your kid', but now she has to find out who she will be when she leaves home. Who does she become when she is no longer your kid, when she has to become 'her own woman'.

In times past most adolescents' sense of identity was determined in large part by their employment. The story is quite different today — as we know, many teenagers are despairing of ever getting a job. No longer do young people have so much choice in regard to work, often they must take whatever they can get. Many simply give up trying to get a job because the continual knockbacks can be so soul-destroying.

A teenager looking for an identity is looking for labels to hang on himself and the more labels he finds, or makes, or is given, the stronger his identity will be. Some kids will borrow labels from others for a while until they get their own set. The people they borrow from may be television or movie stars, pop singers, footballers, criminals, whatever. Some of what they borrow may stay with them for life if they don't come across something better, or if they are not encouraged to create their own identity.

To help a young person build an identity means to help her hang labels on herself. You can help her hang positive labels by providing encouragement or you can help her hang negative labels through insults, discouragement, and sometimes through inappropriately expressing love and concern. Some of the ways you can help a teenager build his identity are quite simple:

- Encourage her to get her own birth certificate and medicare card;
- Encourage him to get his own tax file number and to open a bank account;

- Encourage her to join the library so she gets a library card with her name on it;
- Make up a book containing his school reports, photos, poems he has written, and other such things;
- Encourage her to make up a job résumé which lists her school achievements, interests, hobbies and other skills;
- Display any trophies and certificates he may have won or received in sports or other interests;
- Buy her a wallet and encourage her to carry her identity around with her;
- Hang a sign on his bedroom door stating whose room it is.

All of the above are important in helping a young person establish her identity, and are even more effective if backed up with strong encouragement to take responsibility for herself and develop her own talents.

How and when to let go of the young adult

One of your primary responsibilities, from the very beginning of your parenting, has been to protect your children from all sorts of harm. Protecting your children is such a natural and frequent part of parenting that you often don't even realise you are doing it. Like driving a car, the moves are so familiar that you do them without thinking and without being conscious of what you are doing. There isn't much similarity between driving a car and parenting, other than that much of what parenting involves becomes habit and the more you have become used to protecting, or rescuing, your children the more painful they will find it when the time comes to make the break.

The pain and stress of the breaking away can come in many forms, depending on your attitude and the attitude of your child. It can be painful getting used to standing aside and resisting the natural urge to rescue your child. At the other extreme, it can be painful if you find it almost impossible to get your child to take at least some responsibility for himself rather than relying on you to rescue him all the time. It can be painful for the young adult who must fight to be allowed to fly solo and it can be just as painful if a young person is afraid of being responsible for herself, is so used to being rescued that she doesn't know how to fend for herself.

Some kids suddenly find themselves cut off from both divorced parents who have taken new partners and who don't want the children from the old union. These young people must take care of themselves without understanding why this should be the case. It is also quite likely that they will not have the skills to be able to cope. Many make mistakes and so have to endure the negative labels that 'good' people hang on them. However, that is another story.

'Letting go' of the young adult is the same as saying 'rescuing him less often', and these are the two ways we can look at the problem. The first implies that we need to look at how we are currently rescuing him, how often we should rescue him in the future, when to rescue him, and to what point we should rescue him. The second implies that we need to look at the things we are no longer rescuing him from, how to reduce the number of rescues, how to reduce the size of the rescue, and when to stop rescuing him. This doesn't mean that you eventually reach the stage where you never rescue your children. I don't think parents ever stop being parents, and you will probably go on rescuing your kids in some way for life, without causing any great problem. At adolescence, however, the amount of rescuing needs to be reduced quite drastically, simply because your child's capacity to solve her own problems and to act responsibly is so much greater.

Letting go of your child means handing him full control of his life. As we have seen, this means handing over ownership of his problems, allowing him to solve his own problems, and to take the consequences of his actions. It means showing the young adult that you believe he has the sense to make responsible decisions. Every time you decide to stop rescuing him from certain situations, he is getting your vote of confidence. Getting a vote of confidence from his parents is a great builder of self-esteem for any young person and encourages him to continue to behave responsibly. It isn't hard to see that a positive cycle can be set up in this way, with the young adult getting stronger and stronger with each revolution.

The difficult part for you is to decide when to stop rescuing and in what circumstances, or to what extent to reduce the number of rescues. Our discussion on limits should have helped you decide these things. What needs to be pointed out here is that too often parents unconsciously hang on to their children by continuing to rescue them. All the good work you have put in as far as encouraging your child in decision-making and setting limits can be ruined in this way. This is something you need to be very careful to avoid.

The more that a teenager feels she is in control of the world around her (and limits play a big part in this), the better she feels about herself. And the better she feels about herself, the better she is likely to treat other people. As was seen in the previous chapter, young adults need the security of clear limits and the freedom to control their lives within those limits. The trick for you is to decide what those limits should be and I suggest you decide on them after putting some thought into what you are prepared to stop rescuing your teenager from. There is no magic formula I can pass on about this because all kids, and all parents, are different.

Your teenage son may be a very dependent person who needs a lot of encouragement in all three areas of responsible behaviour. He may therefore need very narrow limits, with only a few things to decide for a while, taking into account his ability and what you are prepared to stop rescuing him from. This is fine as long as you are genuinely allowing him to take control of, or encouraging him to take control of, what he is capable of handling on his own.

Your adolescent daughter may be well aware of her limitations in terms of responsible behaviour and may make your job easy by quietly discussing the appropriate limits of her decision-making. This is the case with a great many teenagers, despite what is said about them in general. Or your adolescent may be someone who wants broader limits of decision-making than he is willing to take the consequences for. This is getting into more difficult waters, because you need to come to some decisions about rescuing him when he goes beyond the limits but tries to avoid the consequences of doing so. You may wish to make the limits a little narrower than he is happy about, knowing full well that he will go outside whatever limits are set anyway.

Your adolescent may be so headstrong that you do not get a look-in until things go wrong, when she expects you to save her. Where the limits are to be set in such a case depends entirely on what you think you can handle. Some parents decide to draw a line and say, 'No more'. Others continue to rescue their child for life and will sacrifice all their money and possessions rather than see their child take the consequences of his actions.

Although children are all so different the general guide when it comes to letting go is to take advantage of your vast knowledge of your child's abilities and needs. Take note of how well she solves her small day-to-day problems, the ones that normally go unnoticed. This will reveal if she is having trouble with one or more of the three parts which make up responsible behaviour.

Rescuing versus responsible behaviour

When I talk about 'rescuing' a young adult I certainly mean saving him from something, not saving his life but saving him from the day-to-day decision-making and responsibilities he faces as he goes about satisfying his needs and wants. The general idea is that, by rescuing, we are saving a teenager from having to learn to behave responsibly and so are preventing him from becoming a responsible and independent adult. Rescuing can occur at each of the three stages of responsible behaviour and one of the major problems with this is that the resentment which builds up from always being 'saved' can cause lasting damage to the parent–child relationship. Such resentment is natural in one who continually feels that someone else is looking after her interests, because it undermines her own capabilities. It may be mystifying to her rescuer, who may believe that she should be thankful for the help. But the point is that it is not help, in the long run. You are dealing with a young person who is biting at the bit, who wants to get on with her own life and be free to make her own mistakes.

The scenario goes like this: The rescued person gets a hidden message from being rescued, which is that the rescuer is smarter than he is, that the rescuer is stronger than he is, that the rescuer is more skilled than he is, that the rescuer is better at seeing problems coming than he is. In other words, although the rescuer may be rescuing the person out of love and concern, the one being rescued is being told that the rescuer is superior in some way.

The rescued person will no doubt be grateful if some real danger existed, which she was unaware of, but even then she may bring up all sorts of reasons why she could not have been expected to handle the situation. This allows her to save face.

As I have said many times by now, parents rescue their

children through habit. It has been a lifelong habit and is seen as being a natural act. Parents do it out of love and concern for their children, yet their children may only show resentment. Other people might even say that they should be grateful for having parents who care enough about them to want to help them out so much. Most parents would probably say that they love their children too much to stop rescuing them and that they will continue to rescue them even if their kids do resent it. I believe that it is quite possible to show the love and concern that goes with rescuing by becoming more selective about when and how it is done. There will be plenty of situations from which your teenager will still need to be rescued, simply because of her insistance on having more freedom than she can handle. Moreover, rescuing can be done in such a way that it focuses on the problems your child is not yet able to handle. It can be done in a way that encourages her to keep searching for the skills, strength and wisdom to handle difficult life problems. Your parental instincts can still be followed but in a way that is appropriate to parenting a young adult.

Unconscious rescuing occurs in the thinking, doing, and consequences areas of responsible behaviour and in each case deprives the young adult of the opportunity to develop. It can also be damaging to the parent-child relationship. It produces either an irresponsible, unhappy child or a resentful, unhappy child. Either way, the parent is usually just as unhappy and may also become resentful towards the child for being so ungrateful.

Rescuing at the thinking stage

Children tend not to think very far into the future, so they often do not see problems coming up. They live more in the present, letting the future look after itself. Most adolescents think that the geriatric years start at twenty-one, and, to them, that's a lifetime away. The trap for you to avoid at this stage is adopting a 'been there, done that' approach. Although you may have experienced a particular situation

LEAVE 'EM TO LEARN

before, you need to remember that for your child it is the first time, which is also a learning time. You may wish to help out because you have been there before, and indeed this is quite natural in a parent, but it does prevent your teenager from becoming aware that he has a problem. The child has been rescued from the feeling that comes with the discovery of having a problem, the feeling that becomes the motivation for solving it. Rather than feeling frustrated that something has gone wrong, your child will feel resentment towards you for presenting him with a problem that he does not own. By pointing out the problem, you are in effect approaching the child with the problem, and we know by now that whoever does the approaching is the person who owns the problem. If you wait until your child becomes aware of the problem himself, then the problem is his, and so the responsibility for solving it is also his.

Sometimes very simple acts like noticing that your teenager's boots are getting a bit worn and supplying new ones will cause her to become very defiant and disrespectful. You may then step up your efforts to please her by bending over backwards to provide everything she needs. You may even take this to the extent that she never has to ask for things because you anticipate her every need. But instead of improving, your relationship only gets worse. At this stage it may be time to back off, to stop anticipating her needs and to allow her to discover that she needs certain things and so she must work out how she is going to get them. Just remember how nice most people can be when they want something, and remember also that it is only her problem if she does the approaching, in order to satisfy some need.

The next trap you must be aware of, at the thinking stage of responsible behaviour, occurs when your child is slow to think up ways of solving a problem and you step in to state what you see as the alternatives, perhaps even before he has had a chance to say anything. If you do this you have rescued him from thinking up ways of relieving the feeling that came when he discovered he had a problem. (If he wasn't rescued from experiencing that feeling.) While there is nothing wrong with you making suggestions once he has run out of ideas, or genuinely cannot think of a solution, care should be taken to give at least two alternatives so he can still make a decision about what he is going to do.

The third trap to be wary of is telling your child which alternative to choose. This rescues her from having to decide for herself, and even though you may think the best alternative is obvious, your child may think otherwise. Her needs may be different from yours, likewise, her ability to carry out the choice may differ. By choosing the alternative for her, you may be setting her up for a fall because she may not be able to cope with your choice. If you push a particular solution and it goes wrong, your child can quite rightly blame you because, after all, you chose it.

Great patience is sometimes needed to allow a teenager to think up possible solutions to a problem and to choose between them, but it does pay off to wait because, as we have seen, it is far more positive to let him take responsibility for his choices in life and whatever they bring him. It may be that his choice seems a bit strange to you, in which case you should remember that he is probably doing his best, that people do not usually deliberately make life difficult for themselves.

Your teenager may be very troublesome, refusing to even think about how she could solve a problem. The simple solution for you is to leave her problem unsolved. If she is one of those kids who believe that, 'No parent can make me do nothin'', she will find that you have come to believe that 'No kid can make me do nothin''. It is, after all, her problem, and sooner or later she will almost certainly come up with a solution, perhaps one that will cause you a problem, but a solution just the same.

So what all this amounts to is that it is possible to deprive your teenager of the opportunity to practise being responsible, for this is exactly what you are doing if you continue to 'rescue' him from deep waters. What you also do is slow up his progress towards becoming a responsible, independent adult. He will not thank you for this; he is no longer a 'child'.

We have seen that other adolescents are quite pleased to be rescued and don't particularly ever want to be held responsible for their behaviour. They seem quite happy being rescued and blaming you for everything that goes wrong. And they are right, of course, because you are responsible if you did the approaching, you thought up possible solutions, and you decided what to do — why shouldn't you take the blame?

While the above comments make it seem all very clear-cut, it is as well to remember that an adolescent will not be one or the other, but will probably swing between extremes. Sometimes she will want to fly solo and sometimes it would take an earthquake to shake her from the nest. She might make very sudden switches between wanting to be very independent on the one hand and refusing to even give an opinion on the other, almost in the same breath. None of this is unusual, just maddening.

Rescuing at the doing stage

The main trap for you to watch out for at the 'doing' stage of learning responsible behaviour is that although you may be able to carry out decisions more quickly and more effectively than your son, you should always step aside and allow him to act for himself. To step aside to allow him to bake a cake is much the same as when he was two or three and you were teaching him to do things like do up his buttons, tie his shoelaces, or comb his hair. You had to stand back and watch as the job was done slower and probably less well than you could have done, but you could see that it was more important to be patient, especially when you saw the smile on his face when he had managed to do it.

You may also have to stand aside and watch as 'mistakes' are made. As I have stressed, you just need to keep on encouraging your daughter to keep trying. You should also be sure to point out the good points in what she did. Even mistakes can be positive if you point out that she has learnt some of the traps to avoid next time. Comments such as 'At least you tried' also provide encouragement and boost her self-esteem. But she doesn't have to be finished to deserve encouragement, which is more valuable when she is trying than when she has won. In sports, the encouragement of fans is used to lift an athlete's performance and it can change a loser into a winner. It is while he is trying that the sound of the cheering crowd rings in his ears and spurs him on to greater effort. Many athletes would find it difficult to rate which is the greatest thrill, holding the cup up high at the end of a race or the sound of the cheering during it. All would agree, though, that winning is very difficult if there is no encouragement to keep trying:

- 'Keep it up, you're getting there.'
- 'Your marks are getting better each time.'
- 'You're doing much better than last week.'
- Compared to how you started you're really doing great.'
- 'You're not up with the others yet but you are improving each day.'

Rescuing at the consequences stage

We talked about this in the previous chapter, but it is so common to see parents 'rescuing' at the consequences stage that it is worth mentioning again. It is hardly surprising that parents find it difficult to step aside at this stage, after all, who wants something unpleasant to happen to their child? No-one, of course, and I mentioned before that it *is* your duty to intervene where serious harm may come to your child. This is something that has to be taken into account in the letting go process. Even though you may have decided to stop rescuing your daughter from the consequences of her actions, you can and should step in if she is in danger. Initially, you may have told her that she is on her own, but now things are turning out even worse than you feared. In this situation you can step in and still maintain the letting go plan, simply by stating that you've only changed your mind because of the unexpected outcome.

Having said all this, in normal circumstances and with problems that are not life-threatening, as much as you may feel like protecting your son by stepping in, try to remember that this would be depriving him of the opportunity to take care of himself. If you rescue him you are, in effect, telling him that you don't think he can be responsible. You should also bear in mind that you are not always going to be around to save him from the consequences of his actions, and that there may be times when others will not allow you to save him from them, for example if he breaks the law. Obviously, it is much better to spend your time preparing him to face the consequences of his decisions.

Parental responsibility versus children's rights

In the very first chapter I mentioned the apparent contradiction in parents being responsible for their children but not having the authority to control their behaviour. As our last topic, we will resolve this issue.

You are responsible for the protection and care of your children. Not many people would argue with this statement so there is no need to explain what it means. What I do want to explain though, is my idea of what you, as parents, are and are not responsible for in regard to the behaviour of your children. Up to adolescence you can, to a large degree, direct the behaviour of your children, therefore you can be held responsible for how your children behave. To put it another way, small children usually allow their parents to tell them how to act because they believe their parents know the best way of doing things.

At adolescence, however, your child begins to withdraw from allowing you to tell her how to behave because she no longer believes you know it all. Consequently, you are no longer able to direct what she does, which means you can no longer be held responsible for her behaviour. Where the small child gives her parents authority, the young adult starts to withdraw from it.

As the young adult withdraws from your authority he must start to take responsibility for himself; the more he withdraws the more he must take responsibility for his own behaviour, like an adult. You have a corresponding change in responsibility and should begin to move into a position where you are responsible only for how you react to him, not for how he acts. An example here will help illustrate this shift: A small child takes her lunch to school each day, and her parents are responsible for this. There has never been any problem with this because she has always taken her lunch without argument. Quite suddenly, though, things change and she refuses to take her lunch. If she does take it, she doesn't eat it — she leaves it in her bag or throws it in the bin. Her parents still feel responsible for her taking lunch to school.

So it is the parents' responsibility to provide the lunch, one that the child likes, and the bag or whatever it is to be carried in; in short, to do whatever is reasonably expected to encourage the child to take lunch to school. Once all this is done the responsibility for eating the lunch rests with the child. As has been pointed out in earlier chapters, you cannot make anyone do anything, you can only influence what they do by the way you act. If you have done what you can reasonably be expected to do in a situation then you have met your responsibility.

A more extreme example would be: Dad helps David to get a learner's licence and buys 'L' plates. He offers to go with his son whenever he can, to give him driving practice. David wants to learn without the 'L' plates but his father refuses to give him the keys. David reacts by 'hot-wiring' and stealing a car, and says he only did it because of his father's earlier refusal. Dad may fall for the trap and feel guilty, that perhaps he is to blame. The real situation here is that Dad has provided all the conditions necessary for David to act responsibly but David *decided* to act as he did, even though he could have reacted in other, more responsible ways. Therefore, it can be put that a teenager must be held responsible for his behaviour when he has the ability and the opportunity to act responsibly and he chooses not to.

Summary

Through being aware of the three stages of responsible behaviour and of your own rescuing habits, it is possible to make a decision as to what part of a young adult's problem-solving needs attention. This is done by setting appropriate limits within which the young adult can develop responsible decision-making, without needing you to come to the rescue. If you have paid attention to helping your teenager build an identity by encouraging her to hang positive labels on herself, there is more chance that she will respond to increased opportunities for responsible behaviour in a positive way.

Naturally, you want to protect your child from harm and may tend to rescue him from experiencing one or more of the three parts of responsible behaviour. This is usually done because you have 'been there, done that', and want to give him the advantage of your experience. You are able to anticipate problems, to think of different ways of solving them, to pick the best ways of solving them, and you may be able to do so more quickly and better than your teenager. Despite all this, you should avoid 'helping out' or 'rescuing' because, as I have stressed, this will not teach your child to be a responsible and independent adult.

If you are rescuing your teenager in the thinking and doing parts of responsible behaviour, then she is justified in blaming you for how things turn out, and you should be prepared to take the consequences if this is the case. Perhaps you are only rescuing her from one of the functions at the thinking stage. For example, you may be rescuing her from having to 'own' a problem, from having to think up ways of solving it, or from making the decision as to which alternative to put into action. It might be that you are only rescuing at the doing stage, or only at the consequences stage, but wherever there is rescuing there is bound to be resentment along with lost opportunity for her to experience what responsible behaviour means. As a parent you need to understand where parental responsibility for your daughter's behaviour ends and her responsibility begins. I suggest that that point is reached when the young adult has the capability to solve any problem which affects her in a responsible way.

Some final remarks

Having read this book, you may decide to 'give it a go for a bit to see if it works'. I strongly urge you not to take this approach because the ideas and suggestions presented here are not 'throw away' things that are tried only for a week or so. Miracles do not happen overnight.

The ideas and suggestions presented will work in the short-term, although they may seem to break down when the heat is really on. Remember that people tend to resort to old and familiar ways of behaving when the going gets tough and this applies to parents as much as teenagers. If you are only 'trying it out for a bit' you will tend to drop back into your old methods of parenting just at the time when it is important to feel confident in the way you are handling the situation. If you are not convinced that a new way of doing things will work, then you will probably only half-heartedly apply it, especially when you are under pressure. As a result you may wrongly decide that the method is no good.

Some teenagers distrust and test adults because of unpleasant and stressful events that have occurred in their own short lives. For example, many have experienced losses that have never been properly dealt with, perhaps because adults believe that 'kids get over things quickly'. Many kids have grieved silently for years over a death, or a family break-up, or the loss of friends, where the adults around them have been too busy with their own feelings to see to those of their children. Some teenagers express grief through misbehaviour born of resentment.

While you may be judging what is suggested here while trying it out, your teenager may be applying the heat to see if you really do want to improve your relationship, or whether, sooner or later, you will resort back to your old ways. Your teenager will be judging you, not the method, and your relationship may suffer a further setback as a result. Even if you are convinced, as I am, that the ideas presented should be used when relating to teenagers, it may still be quite difficult to always put them into practice. I find that I still tend to drop back into old habits when the going gets tough. When this happens I take the opportunity to examine what happened in the hope that I will come to recognise the early signs of slipping back. I have found, for example, that I get a tightening of the jaw as I am becoming upset. When I notice this happening I stop myself from reacting without thinking — I think, and then I say or do something else. This works very well for me and over the years I have come to know what particular situations bring on the tightened jaw. If you take time to examine your reactions, you will undoubtedly find that you also have an early warning system that you can learn to recognise. Very often, it will be some physical reaction which you can feel in your body.

But there are still times when I don't recognise the signs and find myself in a yelling match that takes a much greater effort to pull back from. At other times I do recognise the signs but feel justified in ignoring it, and jump in, boots and all. This is my choice, and I am still making a decision to take that course of action.

Rather than just 'trying it out for a bit', I urge you to give some careful thought to anything you have read here which you believe you could use to build or repair your relationship with your child. You may have to alter your ideas a little about the way you relate to people, but it is important that what you do is *your* way. Remember, you are responsible for how you act as a parent and this includes whether or not you adopt the suggestions mentioned in this book. It is a bit like religion, unless it becomes a way of life that is part of you and feels right for you it has little chance of surviving the tough times. And there can indeed be tough times when it comes to parenting teenagers.

So, if you decide to adopt some of the ideas presented here, remember it will take patience, and perseverance, on your part. Your relationship with your teenager will not improve miraculously overnight, rather, it will improve slowly, as trust between you is built up, and you learn to co-operate with each other. If you put the work in, and are genuinely prepared to 'let go', the rewards will be rich indeed.